I See Better with My Eyes Closed

Conversations with Spiritual Healer, Angel Santamarina

D1714096

Erica Broberg Smith & Angel Santamarina

DEDICATION

To our families, without whom not one word of this book would have been possible.

With our deepest heartfelt gratitude to
Cathy Santamarina, Sofie Santamarina, Nick Santamarina,
Scott Smith, Kyra Smith, and Wyatt Smith

CONTENTS

I See Better with My Eyes Closed

ACKNOWLEDGMENT

I am profoundly grateful to my wife Cathy for introducing me to the spiritual world. From the very beginning when we discovered the Gift I had, she encouraged me to continue investigating and she supported me and enhanced my confidence.

Being able to share my work with Cathy, and her understanding and steadfast presence through this journey has allowed me to surrender fully to the Gift. The luminosity of her soul has enriched every experience and for that I am deeply grateful.

I have also been blessed with the unconditional love and support of my two children. Thank you to Sofie and Nick.

FORWARD

by Erica Broberg Smith

I am suspended in light.

Your eyes (or ears) have a wonderful journey ahead. Angel's Gift entered my life in a seemingly random series of events. It has now lovingly arrived at the doorstep of your soul.

During my first healing with Angel, he said to me, "You must follow the flowers—the path of flowers that lay before you." In my mind's eye, I slid down a slope of soft, fragrant flowers of an inexplicable variety. Many of these flowers were new to me, as I hadn't encountered their natural beauty or fragrance throughout my half-century life. These flowers will be shown to you in the pages ahead.

Angel is a comfortably familiar soul to me. His demeanor is humble and compassionate (unless it's about golf!), and he exudes infinite patience. I have tested that patience with hours of questions, theories, confusion, wide-eyed disbelief, and sometimes flat-out horror. I have laughed and cried and experienced the full range of emotions available to me during the writing of this book.

Months before the idea to collaborate on this book arrived in my mind, a college friend visited after living 20 incredible years as an international peace envoy in places like Rwanda, Darfur, and Myanmar. After a few beers, I whispered to him, "Chris, I need to know—have you ever seen true evil? Does it exist?"

His profound answer, filled with wisdom and compassion, was, "Yes, I have witnessed true evil. However, I have also witnessed the miracles and grace of God."

Looking back, I was already preparing myself, albeit unconsciously, for the challenge ahead of diving headfirst into a world so complex yet simple, which would continually up-end and transform my belief system.

After afternoons spent with Angel, I often lay in bed at night, feeling as though I'd been shot out of a cannon into the cosmos. Many summer nights, I woke up quietly, went into our pebble garden, and gazed at the sky. I cried, sometimes uncontrollably, as I felt overwhelmed by the reality that was being shared with me. I felt and still feel what I can only describe as a "knowing" that what Angel has so lovingly shared with me — and now you — is the Truth. It's as true as the ocean, the sky, or the air we all share.

I would like you to know the Angel that I know. He's a hybrid of an American preppie with wire-rimmed glasses and well-worn boat shoes. He wears a polo shirt with the collar up and a sweater over his shoulders as if he is casually arriving at a polo match. He has the flair of a Latin gentleman, which is evident when he unconsciously sways and pivots slightly as he talks. He's good-natured and easy but becomes animated and boisterous when the topic turns to golf. As fellow horse lovers, I can occasionally stir up his passion for legendary Argentine polo skills, equine athleticism, and spirited Arabian horses.

Our summer routine usually began at 10:00 a.m. on weekdays. He would arrive, I would get him a glass of water, and we'd sit on the covered porch of my cottage, shooing the dogs away who sought to annoy him. Our book sessions started out with us talking about random things—a bit of family, architecture, and world events, but all in a light and jovial tone. I usually received some sort of profound, seemingly unanswerable question in my mind, and sometimes, I dropped it right into the space between us to see if he would play. I would know by the time the last word left my mouth and hovered in the air if he would join in. If not, I would back away in my mind and reach for a lighter inquiry, but in the same vein.

Each of our sessions lasted from 45 minutes to many hours. Some ended crackling with vibrational energy and pure joy in the air. Every day, I felt a deep sense of gratitude as I watched him walk through the gate back to his car.

Other days, after he left, I just sat and contemplated the trees, which were only a few feet tall when I planted them decades ago. They now loom 40 feet above. Some afternoons, I sat with my mouth open in disbelief. Shock, awe, confusion, and a dash of fear danced around me as I tried to compose myself and regain some sort of balance.

My favorite days were the sessions that wrapped up with us both staring at each other in awe about what we'd both just learned. There were days, particularly in the India portion of the book, when I felt the infinite love of Amma pouring into me and powerfully radiating outward from me in a sphere the size of a car. I kept thinking and feeling: Love, Love, Love, Love. For days afterwards, I walked around loving everyone I saw and feeling a deep compassion and profound peace. I felt a connection of love with everyone, everywhere.

There are times when our families get together, and spirituality doesn't enter the conversation. I gravitate to Angel's wife Cathy, who is a statuesque and graceful beauty. She's a strong person with a moral backbone, who can compassionately explain Angel's Gift and practice infinitely better than he can.

Cathy can intuitively identify those who need a healing and graciously facilitates introductions between Angel and the world. Compassionate and resolute, she's present behind Angel, supporting him and his Gift. She is the anchor that lovingly tethers him as he journeys into the cosmos.

I had asked Angel to go deep into the connection between Cathy and himself one day. I wondered if they had journeyed together in previous incarnations. The answer was "yes," then hesitation. Then, he whispered two words, "too personal." Angel works diligently at separating himself as a person from the conduit he serves as a healer. He has the extraordinary ability to compartmentalize these two existences. This separation is essential as he lives quite contently as a family man, happily married with two adult children he enjoys immensely.

There are times I didn't notice at first when Angel's voice changes into a deep whisper with a different tone. It's as if the Gift itself is speaking directly to me since this only happens when we venture deeply into profundity.

There was a portion of the meetings where I was fixated on understanding evil. When we began our meetings, I was of the belief that true evil didn't exist and that it was a fabrication by man. The understanding of the actual existence of evil hit me hard, and I was deeply saddened for days.

During this turbulent time of growth and understanding, I leaned heavily on a few special beings. Our first reader or "test pilot" was Rev. Posy Jackson. She happily volunteered when I reached out to share the book concept and early experiences. Posy remains an eternal hippie, avid naturalist, and quirky ingénue. As a young child and throughout her teen years, she escaped to the dune-swept bay beach of her parents' Amagansett, New York, summer home. She would lounge and search the starry sky, knowing that the place and time she was experiencing were not all that is. Her yearning to see beyond the stars led her to explore spiritual modalities. Yet, her greatest exploration is occurring now in her seventies. It has been a privilege and joy to share this crazy adventure with Posy. Her unwavering support, peppered with the two-word emails, followed up by a call, "Holy Cow!" or "Just Wow!" eased the pressure and responsibility that visited my shoulders daily. Posy departed this Earthly life on February 14, 2023. Valentine's Day, a fitting day for such a loving soul.

After each book session, I would share what I had learned with my patient and supportive husband Scott. He patiently listened to every word and added his input and outlook. I could not have authored the book without his daily support and encouragement – it is that simple. There were times when the sessions were so intense, that Scott would take the children on an adventure into nature for the day so that I could process and 'regroup' and assimilate what I had learned. Scott helped me to balance the book and my personal life, and for that, I feel humble gratitude.

I offer this book to God with indescribable joy and relief as a thank you for all that is and will be. I hope these concepts and ideas will impact you in a transformative way, providing a deeper sense of peace and a clearer path inward within yourself and upward to meet your God.

During this process, I found the key to my own heart, which fills me with a peace that was wholly unknown to me before. I wish the same for you. I hope with love and compassion that I See Better with My Eyes Closed helps you and those impacted by you to find the key to your own hearts.

Peaceful steps,

Erica

INTRODUCTION

"My baby grandson has just drowned!" the woman named Lia screamed in a panic over the phone one Sunday afternoon in Buenos Aires. The boy was one-and-a-half years old and had been underwater for 20 minutes while his mother, unfortunately, fell asleep by their pool.

Lia had been practicing yoga and Transcendental Meditation for decades, so she believed in the power of healing. She only knew of me, however, from my wife, who had been her yoga student. "I contacted all my current meditation students, colleagues, friends, healers, and seers," she told me. "I started prayers and guided meditation groups in the chapel of the clinic, including Buddhists and Rabbis, all united under protection of the Light and Love."

I rushed to the hospital and found the devastated young parents and their friends gathered in the waiting area. The doctors were convinced the boy would remain brain dead. Intuitively, I felt that the family should go to the hospital's chapel and pray together, so I suggested that to them. After all, why waste time waiting when they could actively pray? Meanwhile, Lia obtained authorization for me to enter the intensive care unit to work directly on the boy.

When I perform healings, I receive visions from what I call "the Gift." In my initial vision while with the boy, I was shown an area in the spiritual realm that I understood to be a dedicated place of transition. Souls are lovingly maintained there while their human bodies are unconscious but still alive on earth. It looks grey and flat with no other colors. Lots of bodies were there, neatly lined up. I could describe it as the "Grey Department" with a boss and workers.

As I continued to connect to my Gift, I saw that there was one specific being who was in charge. This being was taller and thinner than the others I'd seen before, and he wore a grey, hooded cloak. He told me directly that he wanted the boy to stay there with him in his department. The other beings who worked in this area also communicated that the boy should stay there, but I vehemently disagreed. I wanted him to return to his life with his parents.

For several days and nights, I visited the ICU and even continued my healing work on the boy while in my dreams. During each healing, I had heated discussions with the grey beings to see if the boy would be allowed to recover his consciousness. I also worked to regenerate areas of his brain that had been damaged due to oxygen deprivation.

One day, I spoke to the parents. I gently and respectfully asked them if they wanted the boy to stay alive even if he was brain dead. They emphatically replied, "Yes." So, I continued to argue with the grey beings that the boy should be allowed to return to his life. It was my will against theirs.

There is a hierarchy of Beings of Light in both good and evil. (There are some on both sides that are more powerful than others.) After several days of arguing with the grey beings, there was still no apparent resolution. Reluctantly, I had to leave on a business trip to Uruguay, but on the third day of my trip, Lia called to tell me he had awakened. The hospital did extensive tests and found there was no evidence of brain damage.

Of course, the boy's healing wasn't my decision or that of the grey beings. It was the decision of the highest power of Divinity. I know that I, as a healer, worked extremely hard, and the doctors worked very diligently, and his family and friends prayed intensely. About two weeks after the boy was discharged from the hospital, I visited him at his house. When I took a moment to connect to my Gift and observe him, I saw that he was a ball of luminous, pure light.

I also had the opportunity to see the boy again several years later. He was four-and-a-half years old by then, and I don't believe he recognized me physically. Nevertheless, he spontaneously ran directly to me at a large gathering, took me by the hand, and led me to the garden to play with stones. I felt this was a Divine acknowledgment that the Gift had played a part in his physical healing. It was a transcendent experience for me.

When the boy was about six, Lia invited me to join them for their weekly lunch at her house. He immediately started to play ball with me and asked his grandmother if I could come every week. For me, this was another beautiful confirmation of our continued Divine connection. The boy is a teenager now, and Light resides within him. I can see it whenever I'm around him. Not surprisingly, his given name is Lucio, which means "Light."

Testimony of the Lucio's Grandmother, Lia:

In 1979, I began to practice transcendental meditation. Shortly after I incorporated hatha yoga, I began guiding meditation and yoga practices and continued that for over 30 years.

One morning in December 2009, the most terrible tragedy happened: the death of my youngest grandchild. My grandson drowned in the swimming pool of his house. The boy was one and a half years old, and they found him at the bottom of the swimming pool. Urgently, his parents took him to the Fleni Clinic just a few blocks from their house. At the clinic, they "chilled" him to slow any activity in his organs. I immediately contacted Angel. I only knew of him through his wife, Cathy, who was my yoga student. She shared with me some astounding accounts of Angel's Gift as a healer. Without hesitation, I called him, and he agreed to meet me immediately at the clinic. I contacted all my current meditation students, colleagues, friends, healers, and seers. I started prayers and guided meditation groups in the chapel of the clinic, including Buddhists and Rabbis, all united under protection of the Light and the love.

The experience with Angel was extraordinary. The energy, consistency, and responsibility with which he acted, and the lack of hesitation in his commitment was profound. Angel had to leave for

Uruguay a few days later, and we coordinated to meditate at the same time in different locations. He worked specifically with the guardian angel of my grandson, who argued that the child had to leave and continue his existence in another dimension.

Angel Santamarina "negotiated" with the Light Being, the child's protector, to allow the child to remain here with his parents. Angel also worked on cleaning his brain because he observed a great deal of damage there. This Light Being, or protector, that all of us have, pressed Angel for an answer from the boy's parents.

So, Angel asked the parents, 'Will you accept your son in any way that he might return?' Angel was referring to physical and mental disabilities or possibly even a vegetative state. The parents accepted that responsibility and said they would accept him in any type of circumstance. Today my grandson, Lucio, is a luminous child as his name defines. He is healthy in every way; mentally, spiritually, and physically.

In the Fleni Clinic, where Lucio had to do a long and intense rehabilitation, they called him (and continue to refer to him) "The child of the miracle." He is now seven years old. Thank you; thank you to the Beings of Light, and those who can communicate with them through the inexhaustible channels of love. Ángel Santamarina is one of them. Miracles do happen!

1 WHAT IS A SPIRITUAL GIFT?

A spiritual Gift is given directly from the Holy Spirit to people to do positive and impactful work on the human condition here on Earth. A multitude of divine Gifts are given to people all over the world and in many capacities, such as hearing, seeing, creating good, and affecting change. When my Gift was bestowed upon me (as you'll learn while you continue reading), it was a complete and utter surprise to me.

As far as I'm concerned, the Gift has been given to me by a Divine source, and I treat it accordingly. No one has told me this, but I feel it profoundly. I can hold it and keep it safe with the respect it needs. I'm merely a facilitator and conduit for the healing energy to flow through, so when I work with the Gift, it isn't me, the human being, who generates the energy or healing.

My Gift also wasn't simply given to me in its current condition. It started with visions, and I had to develop and understand it over several years. It took a tremendous amount of dedication and work to enhance and deepen my connection to the Light, so that I could use it to help others. It required total surrender for the Gift to flourish within me, and it's a practice that I continue to this day.

Divinity doesn't give me a massive telescope to see beyond. It only provides a pair of binoculars that allow me to see more than most human beings. As a result, my reality may be vastly different from yours. In this book, I will only speak about my personal experiences and thoughts from having performed more than 2,000 healings and exorcisms internationally, spanning more than two decades.

You can think of such Gifts in this way: If you stargaze and see a star, you say, "Oh, that's a star." If you then use a pair of binoculars, you can see that there are actually many more stars. If you then use a small telescope, you see many, many more, even though your view is still limited. A giant telescope could show you a galaxy and beyond, but you never know the totality of all that exists, at least from this human viewpoint. Spiritual Gifts are much the same. When I first understood that I had a "seeing capacity," I didn't know I was or would become a Spiritual Healer. But I still, of course, don't have answers that explain the totality of all that exists.

Another way of looking at it is like a puzzle with a thousand pieces. Every healing for me is another puzzle piece, but I don't have all the puzzle pieces yet to get the full picture of 'all that is', and I accept that I will never see the full puzzle completed, at least in this lifetime.

Erica Broberg Smith, who helped me write this book, asked me if I could ask the Gift what it is. This isn't a simple concept to grasp, and every single healing I've done is an epiphany within itself. The universal wisdom that comes to me shows the vast complexity and breadth of the Gift. I have so much reverence for it that I've never investigated where it's from. I wholly and faithfully accept it.

What I See

When I perform healings, I travel beyond this human reality where we dwell. Often, it amazes me. It's an exploration into uncharted territory. My Gift allows me to "see" different timeframes, both past and future, in my mind's eye. I see spiritual realms, and I know with total certainty that they exist. I have witnessed beings that I believe have significance and the power to create a positive or negative impact on people's lives.

'I see better with my eyes closed.' What do I 'see' when I perform a healing? I can describe it as venturing down a main road that has small arteries to turn onto to, but I generally tend to stay on the main road. After years of this vocation, I have developed the ability to turn off the main road and explore, but the most important, primary path is made evident to me. I do ask the Gift, "What is this you are showing me?' Specific images are presented to me by the Gift, and I move through them. If I see you, in the image, swimming in the ocean five hundred feet below the surface, or I see you flying in the clouds, there is a symbolic message there for you.

The Gift is not literally telling me that you are at the bottom of the ocean in physical form. There is information within the visual scene that I need to convey to you to facilitate your healing. The presentation of colors is also integral to my comprehension, since everything I see in black represents something evil, such as negative energies or demons, and if the scene is white with brilliant colors, everything is in healthy Divine order. In the middle area there exist variations of grey, which I interpret as sort of neutral territory. The visions take me on a journey, within which resides the message of the healing.

My healing ability has evolved and developed over the many years, and I now can explore these turns off the main exploratory healing direction if the person I am healing specifically asks me to. If I am asked a detailed question during a healing, I can explore the healing landscape to find information about that specific subject which can then be folded into the healing message. I'm permitted to ask questions to the Divine about the images in order to delve deeper into the information. The images show me the most relevant issues that affect the person receiving the healing at that time. Once the person acknowledges the issues, I'm able to go back to the images and work with new visions that facilitate the healing or reveal the path for resolution.

I always tell people that I prefer not to know anything personal about them prior to their healing. If someone talks about an issue before the healing, they might then doubt what I'm being instructed to tell them. It's much more impactful when I convey information without hearing anything about the person. I can perform healings on my wife and people I know intimately while completely subtracting myself from the equation. Do I have to focus more if I know the person well? Maybe.

I have always felt that what I must do, I will do. I never say "no" to a healing, and I sometimes feel compelled to effect more change. If the person isn't ready or doesn't believe, however, I can't provide effective healing. Still, I have never walked around and switched my Gift into the "on" position to look at the world around me. I only turn it on for a healing. I could be playing golf and sit down on the green at the second hole to perform a healing, if asked. But I don't bother the Gift unnecessarily. If I overused or abused it, would the Gift be removed from me? I'll never know.

I never do a healing after having an alcoholic beverage, as I wouldn't want to compromise a message from the Gift in any way. Maybe I would say things I wasn't supposed to say, or my ego might allow less discernment. How do I live my life as a regular person when I'm not working as a healer? God has blessed me with a wonderful earthly life. I have a loving family and many friends. I love the outdoors and connect deeply with nature.

Over the years, I've created a system of boundaries and parameters by which I perform healings. If all the healing work and the suffering stayed attached to me, it would be exceedingly difficult for me to exist as a person. If something positive happens to the people I'm healing, I remember that I'm not personally responsible for it. Thankfully, part of the Gift allows me to detach from the healing work.

I often think with deep compassion about the people who have come to me for healing, but once the session is complete, the outcome is in the hands of God. I don't encourage people to come to me since I believe a person's healing begins with their own desire to seek it. So, I don't perform healings on anyone unless they reach out to me. I never approach people and ask, "Do you want a healing?" Nor do I say, "I'm going to heal you." I cannot guarantee anything.

Am I overwhelmed by the power of the Gift? No. I'm completely and utterly humbled by it. I have repeatedly been given ample proof of its power. I feel no need to question it, and I know when I'm in that space, everything will be made apparent and available to me. For many healings, I've been led through mazes of images that aren't "rational" to the human mind, yet I fully understand what must be communicated or done.

I have experienced the majesty and intensity of thunder and

lightning within a healing, and I know that God was powerfully present. Such moments are unforgettable. The Gift and I have a sacred relationship. It's a spiritual partnership that has shown me so many wondrous realities, and the only thing I can do is express my deepest gratitude and humility. These pages are a combination of "Divine communications" and "personal" experiences. The purpose of the Gift is to relieve suffering and help others to relinquish their suffering. I could try to look at the stock market in a prescient way and focus it down to a stock price, but I would never succumb to that sort of demand from my ego.

There are times when there is a battle within me to do better and create more positive change. I do have personal feelings about many healings and can get emotional afterwards. I carry with me vivid memories of the many magnificent visions and profound spiritual experiences I've been privileged to witness during healings. When that universal complexity is shown to me, it's truly astounding. In a way, I consider the experiences a private gift for me.

While writing the book, Erica asked me why God doesn't show more people the things I see. The Gift has told me that it's because of the "mystery." It would be too easy for people to know the existence of God right away. The mystery is to be able to go from life on Earth to believing in God without any proof. To have faith. Everyone exists for a reason with their own mission. I always say I don't know if at the next healing, my Gift will go away. If God wants me to do only one more healing, my mission as a healer will be done. I won't question it.

The Purpose of this Book

While in Italy learning and working with spiritual healer Ron Young, a gentleman came to be healed of his longstanding familial issues, which caused him great suffering. His parents had left he and his sister a house as part of their inheritance, and he wanted to convert the house into an orphanage or shelter for the indigent. His sister accessed the deed and sold it without his consent. He was utterly devastated.

During his healing session, Ron and I perceived his pain and asked God for his healing. Suddenly, there was a thunderclap, and brilliant beams of light illuminated all of us in the room. Ron turned to me and whispered something that I will never forget: "If this isn't God, then what is God?"

What are we hoping to accomplish with the writing of this book? We are documenting, expanding, and sharing the message of my Gift with those who are receptive and aligned with the message. More exposure and debate will not undermine the way I see universal existence. Dialogue and discourse are part of our system of beliefs. The act of healing can be transmitted through the act of reading the book, which we have already witnessed with various preliminary readers. Healing works in miraculous ways and the more people that acknowledge this truth, the more amplified Divinity will be within our time-space reality. I think we can all agree that right now, in this moment, more wisdom and meaning is essential.

The purpose of this book is to help people to understand that there is so much more to our existence and hopefully, they will be encouraged and inspired to learn to elevate and illuminate their own soul journey. The more people learn about the Divine realms, the more they grow and transform into fruitful seekers of the 'truth'. There is an inherent peace that comes with the knowing that there is so much more to our existence than this one human life we are living right now.

I have received many Divine communications over the years, and they are never contrary, always clear; and show me aspects of our existence in a particular way. I have never received any conflicting information, so I have a deep sense of knowing that provides balance in my own life, like knowing the sun will come up tomorrow morning. If someone tells me souls do not exist, how should I respond? I know for a fact that they exist. You jokingly asked if I am crazy, or if we both are, as we sit together and discuss a wide range of esoteric topics. If I am crazy, I am consistently crazy. I could accept that angels have wings if I saw them that way, but I do not. I see them as elongated dome shaped Beings of Light. I have seen Ganesh; the remover of obstacles, in the form of an elephant, so I know this traditional depiction is true.

Since I have a spiritual window that I can look out of, I happily share my view with you in these chapters. The goal in sharing this with you is to help you realize that we are all "Light Beings" created by the Divine, and that there's a vast spiritual world we can't see but can access.

For this book project, I must work to recall prior healings and experiences, and not think about them solely with my human brain. My communicating with you is without add-ons or interpretations, and that is why it is not really thinking, and is more of a recalling. When we are collaborating on the book, I feel that it is not Angel talking, but the Gift talking through me. You'll read about some of my experiences as a Spiritual Healer, including my experiences with exorcisms, and I'll consult with the Gift on topics like life and death, love, and hate. I'll also provide a diary of my fascinating experiences in India and observing Bufo venom ceremonies.

Erica assumed she was speaking to 'Angel' during all these sessions for our book since the conversation unfolds in an effortless flow, travelling into extraordinary places, like a meandering river. On the days that we meet, she says the rest of her day is a serene and joyous span of time as if she is floating in a vast sea of tranquility. She feels buoyant, grateful, and humbled. Amazing.

Erica wanted to know why she was drawn to work on this project with me. She asked me to ask the Gift directly. She hopes to be capable and do a sufficient job and feels pressure and responsibility. This is a liberating but daunting task! She worries and prays to be able to compile and convey my insights and the Gift's message for us all.

When I asked the Gift, I was told that our collaboration; its origin, it's…it is a 'call'. Erica is the right person, and it is the right time. It humbles her and she needs this experience. It will make her a better person. This entire process is her soul journey needing more Divine knowledge. It was a call that Erica needed to do this book, which is why she approached me about writing it. I did not have to ask her. If I had asked her, it would be considered work for her. Erica's authentic desire to embark on this intense project is purer in terms of her deeper intention. As I said before today, I know she is the right person. Erica treats it very respectfully, is inquisitive, receptive, and can enrich the overall message. I do not think I could put on paper the fantastic conversation we had today, by myself. So, it is a partnership and a process by which Erica extracts profound information from the Gift, through me. Although many of the answers I gave her I inherently knew, they were not totally obvious facts that I ponder regularly. I must explore to find the insights and meanings. I connect to Divinity and respectfully inquire, 'What is the answer for that question?' It is not that I never knew the answer, or I never thought about it, but that it is not on the surface of my thinking. I must go deep internally to locate the answers to her many questions. The Socratic format of our sessions works perfectly for our project.

Erica asked me what is the origin of a spiritual 'call'? Where does a call come from?

A call is beyond our human comprehension – in a way, it is an intervention, a healing. I told Erica, 'I have never seen anything written by you; yet I trust you implicitly. Connection just happens. You are the person. The only path forward involves your surrender; you need to be steadfast and stop questioning and worrying about your own competence. This experience is an integral part of a profound journey, as you know, and being worried is not productive. You must have faith in the creation that you will be guided. It is the same as if I were worried while performing an exorcism. You are assisting the creation and you are protected. We, together, must depend on God to provide us with the skill, space, and time to create this work. When I perform a healing, Angel cannot be present in the room, because if Angel is in the room he is interfering. If you allow your personal thoughts to interfere with the flow from creation, what you are thinking, asking, and writing may be distorted.'

Why hadn't I created a book like this before in English? Although it had occurred to me, the opportunity did not present itself until now. I believe this is not a coincidence; creation intervened in putting us together so this book could be written. Erica tells me that this process has been such an overwhelming joy for her. Architecture is a wonderful and challenging profession, and she learned so much about how people relate to one another, and about design and the creative process; but she had stopped growing creatively in a significant way about five years ago. She has been searching and praying for something to expand into for some time. She has so much gratitude for our collaboration.

If you think about it, we discuss extraordinarily complex topics. Mysteries that nobody has a definitive answer to, since no person has complete understanding of the totality of what exists. What we discuss are esoteric and irrational subjects that we cannot understand with our human reasoning. The comments I make come to me directly from the Gift. Since I have a spiritual window that I can look out of, I am happily sharing my view. Most people do not have this type of window so I am sharing what is visible to me, in the hope it will heal people, giving them additional faith, and providing them with a higher understanding of spirituality and the larger expanse of our existence.

This book has a higher purpose. The questions and answers are slowly arising as we work. I search inside myself and within my connection to Divinity for the answers and they are provided to me with absolute clarity, then I transmit the information to Erica. The message of the book is neither hers nor mine. All we need to do is propagate this message: 'We want to facilitate the understanding that *there is so much more.*' The message is pure because I do not quote any other person. I am speaking from my own first-hand experience about what I see and perceive. If we attempt to write something with a specific purpose or angle in mind, we risk tainting the sacred message. The person that reads this book can then say what your friend said while sobbing tears of joy, when she read the first draft: 'Wow. All of this does exist. Everything that I thought, and I hoped for is true.' The book will transport the reader where they need to go, in terms of their own healing. The book can pick you up wherever you are in your soul development and give you a broader view of the forces at work in your life. Forces that we may not be able to see or consciously feel. Forces that are working for our greater good and our spiritual growth. If we can apply this wisdom, there can be a profound Spiritual Healing as well as a possible physical one. Our hope is that the book can take readers on a journey that reaches deeper into themselves, and their own Divinity.

I believe Erica's passion for her profession of architecture will be enriched, slowly changing. As her spiritual process expands it will naturally incorporate into her work. She may find she is relying more on her intuition, allowing the creative intelligence to guide her. Erica's ignorance and openness allows her to ask seemingly obvious and basic questions that I would not think necessary to answer. The inexperienced person will be able to comprehend these concepts more easily. This is a good thing. The book provides an awareness of what exists, and it will expand one's heart and mind to this ethereal world, which lays beyond one's immediate reach. The cosmic field is much larger and more complex than you think it is. You will be enriched and make better personal decisions resulting in growth and eternal healing. Awareness is a key part of the puzzle of understanding. How you proceed with your own awareness and how you share it with your family and friends is up to you.

2 THE ARRIVAL OF MY GIFT

Summer of 1999, New York City.

"I saw a man's rotting cadaver looking down at you." I calmly said to the woman lying on the massage table.

We were in a paneled hall with soaring windows and lofty ceilings at the Cathedral of St. John the Divine on the Upper West Side of Manhattan. My wife Cathy had taken me along to a healing seminar.

Cathy was already well-acquainted with most of the group, so she graciously introduced me to everyone. I had just returned home that morning from a business trip to Mexico. I was exhausted, and we barely had time for me to change my clothes and drive to the cathedral. I was a 45-year-old New York businessman (originally from Argentina) with a degree in business management and managing a Wall Street trading desk of emerging market debt. So, what was I doing at a healing seminar?

My wife Cathy had been diagnosed with apparent stage three breast cancer in 1996. She had surgery and was treated with chemotherapy and radiation. She consulted Dr. Mitch Gaynor, an oncologist who was well-known for his integrated approach to treating cancer patients. He suggested she explore healing from Ron Young. After her variety of treatments, her apparent cancer went into remission and she was healed, so Cathy wanted me to meet Ron at his upcoming healing seminar.

Ron was in his forties, tall and lean, wearing blue jeans and a casual shirt. He looked quite relaxed, which surprised me, as I expected someone more formal. He had a pleasant voice and a calm demeanor with measured words, and I could sense his sincerity. Still, I didn't feel he was different from anyone else.

I had never meditated before, so during the group's guided meditations and healings, Cathy suggested I put my hands on my lap. I was to be still and, most importantly, not say anything. There were about 40 people in attendance, mostly women.

Ron lives in both the United States and Italy and dedicates his life to spiritual healing and teaching, working as a healer since he was young. Through the Grace of God, he has produced many miraculous healings with transformative results. Some of his spiritual mentors are teacher and healer Hilda Charlton, Cuban healer Orestes Valdez, who was an expert at removing dark energies, and Dr. Styllianos Atteshlis also known as "Daskalos." From 2005 to 2010, Ron studied with Dr. Bert Hellinger with regard to his groundbreaking concept of "Family Constellations." As a result, he developed his own version of sacred and spiritual family constellations, which go much deeper into historical familial spirituality to heal past generational pain and ancestral suffering.

When we sat down in the room, Ron opened the seminar with an introductory meditation that lasted 15 minutes. Then, a few people quietly brought out a massage table and placed it in the center of our meeting circle. We moved our chairs closer to encircle the table, and Ron very tenderly inquired if anyone desired a healing.

A young woman in her twenties with long chestnut hair and dark blue eyes stood up. She calmly walked over to the table, laid down on her back, and crossed her arms over her chest. Ron started to carefully observe the woman, profoundly concentrating on her, and gracefully raising his hands over her body. He gently moved his hands around and over her before sliding them underneath her torso. He was in some sort of flow or trance, and he moved his head as if he were investigating something in the air with his eyes closed and brow furrowed. When he put his hands above her head, she quietly began to cry. Ron appeared to be doing something, but I wasn't sure exactly what was happening. A moment later, the woman calmed down, and Ron lovingly covered her with a blanket. Then, he addressed the group with a question, "What did you perceive?"

A few people raised their hands and shared their observations about her unhappiness, although most comments were based on what they could physically see. To my own surprise, I raised my hand and shared my own observation about the cadaver. I didn't see his whole body. I saw just the bust with the cadaver's head sort of greenish and decaying with skin loosely attached and rotting. Ron immediately raised his hand up, gesturing me to stop speaking. As the woman slowly gathered herself, he asked her to talk to me privately.

We went to a corner of the room where I shared with her what I had seen in the form of some sort of perceptible vision. At that moment, I didn't have time to process what was happening. She appeared unfazed. 'What you saw is my father, who died a year ago. He's with me all the time.'

"I can tell you that at the end of the healing, the cadaver was smiling at you," I told her. She graciously thanked me, and we returned to our seats. I was shocked and somewhat confused by my observations, as was Cathy, who was sitting beside me. The experience was so spontaneous and unexpected. I didn't consider myself a highly spiritual person or a seeker of the truth at that time at all.

When a second woman, who was in her sixties, approached the table for a healing, Ron started the process again with his hands over her. She also started to cry. At one point, someone asked why she was crying, and the woman whispered, "I'm crying because my dog recently died." At that moment, words came to me, and I felt compelled to raise my hand. "She cried because her mother used to beat her when she was a girl." I said. I described the image of the woman's childhood stone cottage in rural Ireland with her brothers and sisters, and how her mother would violently beat her. (I use the words "I see" because "I perceive" doesn't make sense to me.) I saw the tense family situation and innately comprehended that the anguish she experienced as a child was revealed through her healing with Ron. Her sorrow wasn't about her dog recently dying as she had thought.

After participating in that second healing, I was completely stunned. According to Cathy, I was as white as a ghost. During the break, we went to speak to Ron about what was happening to me. "It's evident that you have a gift or a power 'to see.' You can exercise this Gift, explore, and develop it, or you can ignore it. If you ignore it, it may eventually disappear." It was up to me to decide my path and potential spiritual discipline.

Cathy and I drove back home in reflective silence. Once back at our apartment, I couldn't stop thinking about the mysterious series of events, so I started to investigate it. I called Anna, a physical therapist who had been working for many years with our young daughter, Sofie. Anna was a healer who was trained at the well-known Barbara Brennan Institute.

To our amazement, Anna said she already knew about my "seeing" capacities. She had suspected it for some time. I had previously told her that I recovered from a disastrous car accident as a teenager, which had resulted in paralysis of my left leg. In that tragic accident, my father and I were returning from our cattle farm to Buenos Aires and experienced a head-on collision. I fractured my spine in five places. My father was fine because he was wearing his seatbelt, but I was sitting in an awkward position with my seat tilted way back without a seatbelt. Somehow, I managed to stay conscious throughout the aftermath, but I knew instantly that my leg was paralyzed because I couldn't feel it. I remained motionless in the car for two hours—the worst moments of my life. I knew I had to stay perfectly still because I recalled an accident during a Formula One race when the well-known Argentine driver, Andrea Vianini, was hastily taken out of the destroyed car and placed on the ground. This movement severed his spinal cord, resulting in paralysis. I didn't allow anyone to touch me until the emergency services arrived and carefully removed me from the back door driver's side without twisting my spine. I was transported to a hospital in Buenos Aires and operated on by a talented orthopedic and neurosurgery team who put my spine back together. I was then in a body cast for six arduous months.

While I gradually healed physically, I was destroyed mentally because I feared I would be paralyzed for life. The neurosurgeon said,

"Your knee is like a flan, and you'll never walk again." The comment was so shocking that I made the decision at that moment to cure myself. There was no other option.

I worked diligently for two years. Eventually, I was able to walk slowly without crutches. Even in bed, I pushed my foot against a piece of wood to exercise and strengthen the muscles. This healing work was physical. However, in retrospect, I also needed significant mental and emotional healing. In one of the exercises I created, I dropped my leg to the side of the bed and raised it back onto the bed. I decided that I wanted to set a world record in recovery for this type of accident. It seems so silly now, but I was 20 years old at the time. Plus, it was a positive way to challenge myself. Today, my left leg has 80 percent of its strength with slightly reduced sensitivity due to nerve damage.

As I told Anna about my experience at Ron's seminar, she suggested we try something to highlight my ability to perceive. We sat side by side on the sofa with our eyes closed, and she asked me to tell her what she was doing. 'You're lifting your ethereal body and sitting on my lap,' I told her. I could feel her energy and movement. Then, we tried it again, and this time, I could tell she was returning her ethereal body to her own physical body. A month or so after that exercise, I began to participate in several informal healing groups, trying to understand and exercise my Gift. Members of the healing groups took turns performing healings on each other, and as we worked, visual scenes that were relevant to the person manifested in my mind's eye.

Every healing I observed was filled with information about and for the benefit of that person. I gained perceptions in a newly unfettered way with unprecedented clarity. I began to ask questions about the images I saw, and the answers were instantly made evident in my mind. I could understand the underlying situation and emotions behind the images and scenes. Inevitably, the messages and images I received made sense to the person receiving the healing. I also started reading everything I could about spirituality to try to clarify this power "to see."

Ron Young's Healing Retreat in Italy

In 2000, Cathy and I travelled to a healing retreat in Italy that Ron was leading. Ron and I were able to amplify our energetic spiritual field together as a collective ensemble and perform profound spiritual healings. He continued guiding me to develop and fine-tune my Gift of seeing. His goal is to assist people in finding their own Gifts so that they can enhance their energetic field and become more connected to The Creation.

After receiving scenes and messages during an individual's healing, I would corroborate what I'd observed with that person. I kept a diary of my perceptions of the brilliant imagery of Beings of Light, the occasional presence of evil, and a multitude of other beings and dimensions. I witnessed many aspects of Spiritual Creation, which I'm still learning about today.

In one memorable vision, a woman's sister had died in her arms. Her sister was a nun and very dear to her. During the retreat, Ron scheduled pilgrimages to sacred sites in Italy that continue to hold tremendous energy. One of these visits was to the Church of St. Catherine of Siena, where we meditated in the convent room where St. Catherine once lived. The woman who had lost her sister meditated beside me and silently wept. I intently focused my Gift on her, and I suddenly saw an astonishing image of her sister suspended above us and surrounded by bright light. The knowledge of this filled the woman with joy. She was at peace knowing her sister was now in another dimension as a luminous being.

This experience also filled me with tremendous joy because I could simultaneously connect the vision with the history and a person alive today. At that time, I wasn't calling these interactions "healings," although after each one, I thanked God for allowing me to be a part of easing another's suffering. I asked St. Catherine to help me continue to see these visions and protect me from my human ego. Ron had advised me to never credit my own ego with these extraordinary insights and visions.

We also worked on an older gentleman in his seventies. I

closed my eyes and slowly lifted my arms, allowing the energy to flow from my forehead into my hands to help with my perceptions. I saw the interior of the man's body as the color grey, so I intuitively knew we had to work on a cellular level to cure him from a significant physical illness. I started a process of replacing the grey cells with glowing, healthy white cells. However, I wasn't able to perform this laborious procedure due to the quickly multiplying sick grey cells. This affirmed to me that our efforts were only prolonging his time here but not affecting his earthly outcome. Once I grasped this fundamental realization, I sent him strength to confront his fears so that he would be able to accept his circumstances and destiny, whatever they might be.

My Gift continued to develop while I was in Italy working with Ron. I had a first experience of perceiving someone's past life, and I felt the energy and beings of a specific place and time. The latter happened at the Basilica of St. Clare in Assisi. As I gazed at the painting that showed a deceased St. Clare, I felt goosebumps travel rapidly all over my body. I felt her all-encompassing love and deep humility so vividly that I felt her presence there with me. I leaned back against the cool stone wall and enjoyed the moment, enveloped in infinite love and tenderness. I understood that through her simplicity, her gift was to radiate love, joy, and peace to others.

Later, when we visited the Santa Maria degli Angeli, I had another intense experience. In the interior, there is a small room where St. Francis died on October 3, 1226. Today, it's a gated chapel called the Transito. When I arrived there, I instinctually grabbed onto the gates with both hands and closed my eyes in contemplation. I was swiftly transported into the past and could see and feel St. Francis' infinite love and compassion for all humankind. An image of his death scene entered my mind. I could perceive the cold and windy day and a humble structure that resembled a stable. Two monks were present with some animals, and when one monk realized the magnitude of the moment, he quickly ran to the town of Assisi to get advice about St. Francis' impending death.

Due to the detail and intensity, it's a challenge to accurately describe this series of visions to you. Internally, I asked my Gift why these specific images from 800 years before were being shown to me. Slowly, I walked back to the entrance of the church and rested against a tall column. A flock of white doves suddenly flew in front of me, and I began to cry tears of untethered joy. I turned around, and on one massive wall, I saw a painting that depicted St. Francis at the precise moment of his death in an elaborate bed surrounded by royalty. I knew that his death hadn't been at all like that magnanimous depiction.

When I returned home from Italy, I read about the death of St. Francis. Apparently, when he knew he was close to dying, he called Father Leon and Father Angel and asked them to sing the canticle of Brother Sun. He had told them that when they knew he was about to die, they were to lay him naked on the floor and let him die like that. Through these experiences in Italy, my understanding of Divine power and spirituality expanded. I felt as though an unknown part of me had been illuminated through Divinity. My human life remained untouched, but my spiritual life was completely transformed.

My spiritual life began to expand after the trip to Italy. I felt compelled to investigate my recent experiences. I had heard that many people, after a personal problem or trauma, convert themselves into 'Seekers of the Truth'. As humans, we often do not know what we are seeking, however there is a desire within us that pushes us to continue searching for the mysteries of the infinite truth. The process of spiritual growth develops in a parallel field to our human lives. There are stages of spiritual development that are not consistently timed or linear, because of the interference of our daily lives, and because most of us do not live in a cave in Tibet, immersed in our own personal Divine discipline.

Being a Seeker of the Truth

There are months that pass where we inwardly feel nothing particularly extraordinary, and we feel we do not grow, and then suddenly an experience, book or conversation can illuminate our thinking. Our growth process is not linear and has flashes of intense understanding. In many surprising circumstances, you can meet new people and instantly begin a profound dialogue. There are a lot of human beings who go through this process in silence, and if we delicately observe, we can find like-minded people in these situations creating connections everywhere. Therefore, beautiful and revealing encounters can occur that were meant to be. Set in motion by whom? Casually? Perhaps a coincidence? I do not think so. The essential part of life as a 'Seeker of The Truth' is to remember that the meaningful aspect is the 'search' not the 'destiny', you never really arrive at the end, since absolute 'Truth' is infinite, nor is the search for Truth limited by your age or a certain stage in life. Our true journey is about enrichment and growth, and our search is altogether personal and requires our deeply intimate dialogue with God.

Healing of the Elderly Man

An eighty-year-old man came to me for a healing on his knee and we talked for quite a while during the session about spirituality. He left and came back a week later. When I asked about his knee, he said his knee was the same, but that he wanted to keep learning about spirituality. Our conversation had impacted him profoundly, he was well into his eighties and a new door into the spiritual realm was opening for him. The desire to explore spirituality can occur at any moment in a person's life. Some people are seekers of the truth from a youthful age while others take an interest only with the proximity of death, as they prepare for their seemingly mysterious and imminent transition.

3 WHAT IS SPIRITUAL HEALING?

There are different modalities of healing, such as Reiki, acupuncture, massage, and countless others. Energy healing techniques are typically about "moving" energy, opening energetic paths in the body, or transferring energy through the healer to the recipient. These techniques can generally be learned. In my own work as a Spiritual Healer, I trust that the person receives the healing that creation has determined they need at that precise moment. In my experience, healing always occurs. "Curing," on the other hand, happens when there's an accompanying physical manifestation of the healing.

Of course, when a physical sickness is cured, that's a much more miraculous situation. But it's important to note that curing is the removal of a disease, while healing isn't the same as curing. A cure means a physical illness is thwarted and its progression is stopped, which is more obvious than a healing because we can see a material difference from before to after. If someone passes away in peace shortly after a healing, does that mean the healing didn't work? Certainly not. The karma was already well-established, so the trajectory and outcome of that illness couldn't be altered. My hope is that the healing relieved the fear of imminent death and made the transition to the non-physical world more fluid and peaceful.

For example, in Argentina, there was a woman named Jesus who had suffered tremendously from cancer for more than a decade. Interestingly, an image of Jesus Christ came through to me during her healing session. He was in pain as he carried the cross, and I could see that this woman's pain was similar to Jesus' pain. She was a devout Catholic who saw her intense pain as suffering in the same way as He did. Her cancer was her cross.

"You suffer as Jesus suffered bearing his cross. You suffer and bear your cancer," I told her. At the end of the healing, I saw three crosses on a hill and knew that this was the death of Jesus. I realized that this woman's death was imminent. The moment she heard I had seen the three crosses; she understood the outcome of her journey and that her suffering would soon be over. I learned that she died two weeks later in peace and with a deeper acceptance of her death. It was a very profound, moving, and powerful healing that I will always cherish.

But let us say a person is cured of cancer and survives. They may have had chemotherapy and surgery. Then, suddenly, they are completely cured and cancer-free. We can't assume that a healing session is the absolute cure, as it would be unfair to the doctors and others who helped. We can reasonably assume that a healing has cured someone if that's the only treatment they receive, but not otherwise.

The Anatomy of a Healing Session

Light is a spiritual tool. As humans, we have lost the use of spiritual Light over the centuries. I read and learned about Light from the Bible, where it's described as "Divine Light." Divine Light has the miraculous power to protect, heal, and create action. I always start a session by explaining what I do, but the healing has already begun at that point because much of what I say is particularly relevant to the individual I am working with. I tell them I don't need to know why they've come to see me. I provide examples of other healings, which are often somehow connected to this person's healing and experience. Once I know they're comfortable with the concept, I proceed with the formal opening of the healing, which involves sitting across from one another, closing my eyes, and raising my hands and palms toward the person.

Most healings are about gaining knowledge that will be helpful in this lifetime, but some sessions are purely spiritual in nature and extraordinarily complex, esoteric, and "irrational" in that they aren't of the rational mind. I see images that are pertinent to that person, and depending on the image, its context, and color, I can understand the issues the person faces. I stop and tell the person what I've perceived,

31

and they normally identify with the issue. Then, we continue with the healing until it's finished, at which time the person usually has questions.

I respectfully inquire of the Gift to provide clear information to me, and I can somehow interpret this information to find the essence of its meaning. I'm not passive during the healing; I work to understand and relay the message. If I see someone screaming in my vision, for example, I don't just tell them that. What good would that do? I investigate the context, colors, pain, and fear. I actively ask the Gift, "What are you showing me?" When I'm shown a new image, my questioning continues, and all the while, messages arrive that relate to each image. Eventually, I have a full understanding of the issues and what needs to be done to address them. So, when I talk to the person about the source of their anguish and how to release it, it may not even be relevant to tell them that I actually saw them screaming in my vision.

In general, I don't see an entire life laid out before me, but I see snapshots that are relevant. I could see a child on a tricycle, then a father leaving a marriage, or children within a general timeline showing points of interest. The vision starts where it starts, and it could even be a past life or an image of the future in this life.

Erica has asked me if a person ever looks older when I see them in the future in my visions, but I don't see details of their features. I see situations in their future. I might see a person floating over a grass pasture while leaving the city behind. I'll see brilliant emerald-green as the person goes to a grassy meadow. I might see the person happily speaking with friends in a small town. Those images show me that the harmonious future of this person must be in a different environment.

If only one issue arises within a session, it doesn't mean there aren't also other issues, of course. The Gift knows exactly what needs to heal and focuses on that area at that moment in time. A year from now, this person could have a completely different healing. I never leave a healing unfinished, yet I never know when it starts or when it ends. I have to dedicate the necessary time to organize the information in a particular order, carefully present it to the person, and make sure they comprehend it.

Sometimes, it takes a long time for the person to feel reassured that what I'm communicating is the way to resolve their issues. For this reason, I always repeat the instructions many times until I know the person has fully grasped the concepts. I conduct a follow-up afterwards to unwind the healing with more explanations, during which I'm continuing to perform healing. In many cases, we are talking about the unseen spiritual world, past lives, a connection with childhood, looking at the future, and other things that most people don't have the ability to see clearly. I help each person interpret their thoughts and incorporate the vision into their current reality. People are also welcomed to call me later with more questions.

Afterwards, however, I may never learn of the full effect of the session. I know and trust that what I did was inherently good because the Gift provided the tools to help someone heal. In order to be healed, however, people must believe that healing is possible. There are patterns of domination, abuse, or addiction that aren't easy to relinquish, and some people refuse to change their patterns. Often, people are more comfortable with the familiar, even if it's to their detriment. Their human free will decides their course of action. They can ignore the advice, address it immediately, or address it slowly over the course of many years.

The sanctity of a healing is paramount, and no two sessions are the same. The information I receive comes and goes, and I don't keep it in my memory. I trust the information I receive one hundred percent, not ninety nine percent. 'Angel' the person, does not intervene in the healing process. I do perform healings on children if a parent contacts me to set up the healing and stays nearby during the session. While I don't share the details of anyone's healing with another adult without explicit permission, I will share the details of a child's healing with their accompanying adult.

Non-Physical Healings: Emotional, Intellectual, & Spiritual

I have performed many healings on people who have carried negative feelings all of their lives without an understanding of the source of their suffering. Such a healing happened years ago when I was still working in finance in New York City. A colleague asked me to perform a healing on a woman at his office. She shared her lifelong struggle of emotional suffering with me. Although she was a vibrant and beautiful young lady, she carried intense pain inside and never smiled. During her healing, I witnessed a scene of a loving mother and young child, and then saw the mother dying. A long, dark road emerged that led to her life today. As I prepared to send her healing Divine Light, a Divine Being appeared to me. "Who are you?" I asked. "I am La Madre de todas las Madres (The Mother of all Mothers)" was the answer. This mother proceeded to embrace the woman I was healing. The woman felt the Divine Being's presence, so I instructed her to "allow this Light Being to fully embrace you." When a Divine Being manifests during a healing, it's magnificently beautiful. The 'Mother of all Mothers' being came to embrace her so that she could release her suffering due to the loss of her mother at such a tender age and move forward into the future, leaving her darkness and pain behind.

During one interesting healing, I saw a vision of a man trying to untangle a ball made of stiff iron cables. They were tangled together, and the man was frantically struggling to untangle the knots. The message, "it's an impossible task," came to me. I told him what I saw. "You won't be successful with this project," I said. He then told me his company was going bankrupt, and he was desperately trying to save it. But on a deeper level, he knew he couldn't salvage it. I consider this a type of emotional healing that released him from his despair about his impending business loss.

Intellectual healing occurs when someone "thinks" about a situation incorrectly, and that causes them suffering. They essentially need to be enlightened with the correct information and change their thinking pattern in order to move forward. As another example, if someone is possessed by dark energy, asks for a healing, and then feels they're no longer possessed, we can say the healing cured them of that spiritual affliction. This would be considered a "curing" of the spirit.

Here's an example of a session that was a combination of emotional and spiritual healing and included a vision from a past life.

In New York, I did a healing on a chronically depressed

woman in her fifties and saw a massive black hole or black stain over her heart center. I told her I saw this obstacle on her chest. She told me that she had felt pain over her heart center all of her life. I worked extremely hard, focusing, and trying to remove or open that heavy cover on her heart and finally, I was able to break it open, and go inside. Once past the darkness the scene that came to me was in the Middle Ages, showing me a rickety donkey cart pulling a wooden cage with prisoners within it. She was trapped in that cart and was brought out and decapitated in front of a crowd. I then understood that her soul had gone through the severely traumatic event, and she was manifesting the anguish in the current lifetime as a painful, black, spiritual scar. I knew I had to work with Spiritual Light to remove the black mark and then heal and regenerate the area of the heart center. It was made evident to me that the circumstances of her past life had somehow carried over, and were still affecting her soul today, impacting her current human experience.

Physical Healings

Physical sickness is something that comes into the human system from outside that does not belong or when something internal stops working correctly. It is a negative manifestation from a crack or break in our immune system. I see this system as connected webs of living Light that extend from the top of our head down through every part of our body, constantly absorbing information. When someone is suffering from stress, this web of immunity is weakened, and the system loses its balance. This allows sickness to penetrate the physical body.

I have performed healings on people who don't yet have any physical manifestations of illness. But I've told them that I sensed some imbalance in their body and asked them if they had any symptoms in the area where I detected the issue. If someone has a terminal physical illness, I don't always see the end of their life. I work to physically heal the person and change the outcome to allow for a longer, healthier life. I know that the person wants me to cure them, so I work as best I can to affect the physical outcome on their behalf. There are times when the lifetime outcome is already written as part of destiny, which cannot be changed.

I can perform my healing work with the actual living cells of the human body. I go in deeply and see the cells closely as they reproduce and move around in real time. I work slowly and carefully, taking the dark cells out with my ethereal hand. I move them away from the body and replace them with the healthy Light-filled cells. The new cells are created through my Light Being, the Light of God, and the person's Light Being in the palm of my hand. (I'll explain these Beings of Light in more detail shortly.)

I can't transform sick cells, which is why I replace them with newly generated healthy cells. The sick cells are constantly regenerating, which is why the disease continues to progress. I can see them growing and reproducing in real time as I work, which is frustrating. They grow and multiply as I remove them. Physical healing is a complicated and time-consuming procedure. Sometimes, I can't effect any change because there are too many infected cells to remove, and they reproduce faster than my ability to replace them.

If I see a tumor, I work on shrinking it. A tumor appears to me as a solid black object, and I work with Divine Light like a laser along its edges to make it smaller and turn its perimeter pink and healthy. I work to reduce it in size almost as if it's made of malleable clay. This way, during surgery, the doctors can remove something much smaller. There are people who have found that their tumors had reduced in size after our healing work together.

I then teach the person how to continue the process with self-healing. I can do this work remotely, but it's stronger and easier in person. With remote work, I can't see all the other important things that I would like to see. But of course, working in person isn't always an option. I worked consistently with a man in Argentina named Eduardo for two years via video calls. I consider him to be a living miracle. He has an aggressive form of cancer in his spine and bones. I visualized his spine and saw that some cells were black and diseased, and I work with my etheric hands to remove and discard those cells. I visualized them replaced by glowing white, healthy cells. I also taught him to visualize this process for his own self-healing. Together we examined his tumors in this way and simultaneously worked to shrink them.

One of his subsequent medical analyses was disappointing, so I instructed him to focus deeply and work diligently on self-healing as we continued our work on video calls. His next analysis was much better, so his doctor recommended he continue our healing practice. Even though he still had cancer, he was doing much better physically and had changed a great deal spiritually. He spent much of his time left helping others in the hospital where he received treatment.

When I traveled to Argentina in March 2020, Eduardo wanted to meet me in person, after doing many remote healings together. During my visit, he introduced me to a young woman named Barbi, who had been a long-term patient at the hospital. She had no stomach and was waiting for a transplant. The procedure would be extremely complicated, and she was very frail and thin despite the fact that she was quite young. I worked with her once in the hospital but could tell she didn't have the stamina to focus on self-healing.

Eduardo was heartbroken that she wasn't doing well. "Barbi's story isn't your story," I told him. "She has her own life and destiny, and you have yours. You can't get attached to her story. You can be with her and have compassion for her but maintain your energy for your own self-healing." Sometime after our many healings, his family notified me that Eduardo had died in a very peaceful way.

What follows are some examples of healings that specifically involved Light Beings. There was a young boy in Argentina who was quadriplegic from birth. I performed regular healings on him and saw Light Beings around him. I told his mother, and she would whisper "angels" to him, which would make him smile.

One day, I saw many more Light Beings gathered around him than usual, and it looked as though they were celebrating in pure joy. I knew intuitively that they were there to celebrate his imminent transition and return to God. Two weeks later, he died. I visited his mother a few hours after his death and stood over his body. I put my hands up, closed my eyes, and connected. There was nothing there. All I saw was complete darkness. The Angels had already taken his soul, and all that was left was his physical body. I told the mother, "The Angels have already taken him." I had never seen a case where a large group of Beings of Light prepared so joyously to take a soul on its journey and did it so quickly.

In another case, a desperate man asked for a healing because he felt trapped and claustrophobic. I was shown a serious physical altercation in one of his past lives. I saw two Greek semi-Gods fighting, and one brutally defeated the other. The winner cast a woven net across his captive. In this lifetime, the man somehow felt that net still around him. Then, I witnessed a Divine Being arrive and cut the net, setting him free from his suffering. It was a beautiful and dramatic scene I will never forget. I love being permitted to see and understand these visions, and I'm so grateful for my journey with the Gift.

Self Healing

The Exercise of the Sun

You can learn to use the Light for your own healing. The Light will come to the top of your head and slowly cover your entire body. Initially, you may have to use your imagination for this. I sometimes use the example of how the sun's rays feel when you go outside, close your eyes, and feel it on your face. The Divine Light isn't warm like the sun, but it's luminous. As you practice it, you'll begin to sense it without having to imagine it. The most powerful Light comes from God, and you connect to it through your Being of Light. When you're indoors, visualize Light coming from your Light Being to you. Ask it for Divine Light.

Once you can feel the Light, you can direct it to slowly cover your body from the top of your head to your feet. Imagine your body covered with a cupola or sphere of Light. This is for general protection from bad energies or toxic interactions/situations. You can even protect yourself before you engage in a meeting. I recommend doing this exercise every morning and night. Some days you may feel a stronger connection to the Light than others. You can increase your access with repetition.

If someone has a serious illness, Ron Young recommends that they practice self-healing three or so hours per day. The reality is that we have absolutely nothing more important to do with our time than healing our physical body if we have a life-threatening sickness.

One of the messages that I frequently hear in a healing is "You must commit to changing old patterns in your life in order to properly heal." This was illustrated dramatically when a middle-aged woman who had been diagnosed with terminal cancer came to me for healing. I was directed to tell her to dedicate more daily time to connect with God, work less, and devote several hours a day to self-healing. "I'm too busy for that," she told me. "I have too many responsibilities." Well, she's no longer with us.

She lived her entire existence on the material human plane without exploring her spirituality. She did not have time to save her own life, which is why she departed. I can explain to people what I see and what action they need to take. But if they choose not to act, they won't experience the healing they seek.

I recommend bringing Light to your etheric hands, which are your energetic, powerful hands rather than your physical hands. Imagine Divine Light coming through your forehead, down through your arms and into your hands. You can direct your etheric and physical hands toward the area of sickness, such as a tumor in the stomach, on yourself of someone you love. Move to the edges of the tumor, which are black and grey, and start to shrink it by allowing healthy pink tissue to grow into the tumor. The black cells need to come out of the body and disintegrate. You can pull them out in whatever way you want. It's your intention that matters most. Then, imagine replacing the dark, sick cells with Light-filled, healthy cells. If the cells are metastasized, you can still remove them with Light energy. If you don't think this can be done, ask yourself how you know it can't.

People with cancer are often faced with chemotherapy. There are two mindsets regarding this. They can anticipate that it will be a terrible experience and prepare by thinking about how the toxic substances will make them sick, ugly, and in pain. Or they can look forward to it and thank the universe for this marvelous cure. They can plan to be there fully present, helping to guide the lifesaving chemicals to areas where they're needed and removing unhealthy cells to make room for the healthy new ones. Which mindset is better?

If a child has a stomachache or headache, you can place your etheric hands onto that part of their body, connect to your Light Being, and ask for help in healing them. Make the Divine Light come through your arms and hands and start working to dissolve the pain with Light. As a healer, you're working to reduce and remove the pain.

Some families need a cupola of Light protection around the entire family. I teach every family member to use the Protection of Light. You can also protect yourself and then focus on the group protection of the family. It's an effective way of healing that you can even use when you're physically apart. All you need to do is focus on the Light, but it does take practice. Just know that you are much more powerful than you think you are!

Be Discerning When Choosing a Healer

When you decide to see a healer, be careful about the one you choose, as some can do more harm than good. I worked long distance with a woman named Kay in Dublin, who came to me via a connection with Erica. She had been ill for decades with fibromyalgia, depression, overwhelming sadness, and chronic physical pain. She spent many months at a time in bed and had seen countless doctors with no solutions. Her quality of life was still deteriorating, and she also felt isolated with few friends, which deeply saddened her.

During the healing, I saw her face contorted and full of suffering. My vision immediately went to her stomach. I could see a greyish sort of eel, although not a literal eel, swimming in a circular pattern. There were some yellow stick-like things in her stomach that I understood to be a nest. It was evident to me that I had to get it out of her. "Look upwards and open your mouth." I instructed her. I started working to push this creature out upward through her throat. It was arduous to get it to leave, but it eventually came out of her mouth. I then cleaned up the nesting material by throwing it all up through her throat. I used my ethereal hands to scoop and push the material up and out.

I could see that Kay had undergone some sort of treatment that included something to drink in a type of ceremony, and it was supposed to help her. The intentions were probably good, but this drink had a negative spiritual essence that created a non-physical spiritual affliction within her. Kay had previously done a Reiki healing session, during which she felt something in her throat that wanted to come up. The sensation was almost a choking or gagging feeling, but it never came out.

I taught Kay to work with Light to heal her own stomach, since I saw etheric scars and wounds there. When I did another remote session with her a few days later, her face had dramatically changed. She was happy, light, relaxed, and open with no wrinkles on her face. She said she had been released from her suffering.

Testimony of Kay: The healing and removal of the eel.

There was something wrong, but it was hard to put a finger on it. I felt off. All the time. For such a long time it was, and still is, hard to determine when it first started. This sense of being afflicted, a constant unease. There was shame because I have been blessed with good fortune too, a good family life, financial security etc. Just an inability to get off the ground and eventually a crippling lack of confidence because I was not resilient enough. Physical maladies were constant, I had panic attacks, social anxiety, depression, IBS, existential angst, and a series of complaints that made me feel that I was high maintenance or too self involved.

Not an unhappy person before, but constant dread and that feeling that you cannot cope is undermining, especially after an extended period. Events or experiences that should have been joyful, were instead fearful. Eventually I resisted planning events because I knew that my health would just sabotage any plans. Not a good companion really. Friendships suffered or disappeared. My birth family ostracized me. I felt that I misrepresented myself. I was not who I was or had been. Bad things happened to me. I had a car accident. It took me a long time to recover, then I developed migraines which occurred with frequency. I felt unable to parent. I worried that I would infect my children.

I had a shamanic reiki healing session in 2020. That was the first time I saw something within me. It unfurled from deep within my belly and came up my throat. It was dark, black, and slick. I dealt with this apparition by telling myself it was positive energy, but in truth it was not.

A web of coincidences brought me to Angel. My husband met Erica in France. Perhaps Angel could help me. Nothing so far has really dealt with the malaise. Conventional medicine has offered no relief for the physical ailments and despondency. Maybe Angel could help. I also thought, maybe he couldn't. This was just me. We had a zoom call. I didn't see or feel this creature during that call, but Angel did. Like a big, dark eel. Malign, a poisonous tenant within.

Since its removal., I have felt different. Initially it alarmed me that someone I had encountered had brought me such injury, intentionally or otherwise, and that it could happen again. I know that Angel recognized the cause of my affliction and healed me. I can work toward a full recovery because I can once again depend on myself. I have started to feel that I can shape my life. My IBS has gone. The world is a complex place, I hope that I can do something that brings forth light somewhere.

Testimony of Dylan, Kay's Husband: The healing and removal of the eel.

I am extremely glad to give you an update on Kay. After Kay's healing with Angel, she was, as you know, exhausted - like deep fatigue. Then she noticed that her digestion problems were easing and then for a few weeks went away. I know she worked as Angel advised to continue with self-healing. For the most part, the heavy migraines have gone though she was already starting to manage those. I suppose you could say though that the symptoms of a systemic poisoning have been lifting.

From my perspective close to Kay, I have noticed definite improvement. Some days, before the healing, although Kay would try hard to overcome or work around it, there was a weight/shadow pressing down on her. She became resigned to so many days like that and that was sad. But, in a way that is really noticeable, that same shadow is not cloaking her. Now I feel she can direct her day better. Steer it towards the light if she wishes. That takes practice and perseverance, but I believe that option has emerged.

Healing of the Woman with Open Akashic Records

I once did another healing on a woman who was very confused spiritually. She felt she was in chaos. She told me she'd had an Akashic reading the week before. The Akashic Records do exist and contain the record of our past incarnations, as well as the written history of our souls from inception. I could see, however, that the person who opened the doors to her soul records accidentally left them open, which allowed other entities to enter her soul's space.

I worked to safely seal her records behind what appeared to be two heavy doors. These examples show that we must be careful when we ask for spiritual help. We cannot know how much skill and respect a person has with their access to the spiritual world.

4 THE DIVINE KINGDOM

I have seen specific parts of the Divine Kingdom, which include the Amphitheater of Light. There are different areas of the spiritual world, and I only see small parts of them. The complexity of what I see also makes me think that the totality is beyond anything I could possibly imagine. For example, I have seen a very luminous area filled with spiritual beings, and I believe God is there. At the bottom of this area, I've seen the floating amphitheater that would have been big enough to hold millions of people. There were terraces with Divine Beings observing. From below this floating structure, I have seen the souls coming and going to and from their missions in the universe. That could be what we refer to as heaven, but I don't really know.

I have also been shown a variety of areas for specific purposes, and new areas are often shown to me occasionally during new healings. My knowledge continually expands. It must be similar to how an astronaut feels when exploring outer space.

We each have one specific Light Being who accompanies us and cares for our soul during our human life journey. Many people refer to this being as a "Guardian Angel," and we have direct access to this Light Being even though most of us aren't aware of it. Our Light Being is there to assist us in the transition to and from human life beginning with our soul's arrival into the fetus and the soul's eventual departure from the human body during the process of physical death. When we die, our body stays behind, and the soul continues its journey, accompanied by the Being of Light as a Divine protector.

I don't call Light Beings "angels" since I don't see them with wings. I usually see them to the left and slightly above the person. Probably sometime in history, an artist depicted angels with wings, and it stuck. We gave them wings in artwork so that people could understand the overall concept of hovering or flying above us.

The Light Beings and Divine Beings that I see are from many religions, and they are all part of Creation. I see Divine Beings that are superior Beings of Light with a more powerful presence, but their names are rarely revealed to me. They are an integral part of some healings I perform, but they aren't always present.

Accepting Spiritual Concepts

As I explained all of this to Erica during the writing of the book, she found it difficult to make sense of it all in her mind. She said, "I feel like I'm in a dark room feeling my way around. I'm trying to relate what you're telling me to the physical world I know, but it's impossible since there's no frame of reference that ties them together. We are exploring topics that are 'other-worldly.'"

I answered that this subject is irrational and out of the realm of human reasoning. Your reasoning cannot accept what I'm sharing with you, so you're battling with the reasoning of your mind without hard scientific facts. It's difficult for you to understand and difficult for me to adequately explain the complexity of it. The spectrum of colors, the identification and replacement of damaged cells, the encounters with Beings of Light—it's all magnificently complex. My advice is that you cannot think about these concepts with your rational mind. You must surrender and accept that the whole reality isn't as it seems. There is so much more!

Now that you've read about the Divine Kingdom and Beings of Light, it would be helpful to know more about the 'Journey of the Soul'.

5 THE JOURNEY OF THE SOUL

Every human being has a soul, which is the same as the spirit. It exists regardless of someone's religion or lack of religion. The soul is shown to me as an amorphic form of opaque white. It doesn't have a human shape or features, but it can have a linear volume much like the shape of a human body.

I have come to understand that each soul comes to Earth for a specific purpose. The soul assignment to each specific human is preordained by Divinity.

'The soul is assigned to a human life with love.'

Erica wants to know if souls venture into other life forms here or elsewhere. A soul's first human incarnation is not always its first point of existence; we do not know where it had been before. Souls can travel to places we cannot even begin to comprehend.

Erica is curious about the timing of when the soul comes from Divinity to begin its mission in a human life and if I have seen it enter the body? She wants to know when exactly does this happen? This is such a charged question as it ties into the political debate about the 'beginning of a life' debate, abortion, and religion.

I have never witnessed the moment a soul enters a human form. I can tell you that babies are very pure full of Spiritual Light. I have done numerous healings on babies. Babies are pure Divinity of different degrees and I observe them as pure unadulterated Divine Light. After time on Earth passes, the baby matures, and the experience of human existence begins influencing them and often reducing and limiting their Light. I have never really investigated when a soul enters the human body. At some point, after conception and before birth, the soul attaches and enters the physical body.

The soul does not occupy actual physical space, which may be confusing to understand in terms of a fetus. When I asked the Gift, a very divine, higher level being arrived, and told me that assigning the souls to bodies occurs at varied times, closer to conception than birth. There is a physical formation already, however, the most important aspect to understand is that there is not a particular period pinpointed that every single soul enters the womb. It is assigned specifically and uniquely for each human, at various times in utero, and happens when the soul is instructed to enter by powerful Divine Beings. I was shown that a specific soul waits alongside the newly pregnant woman, awaiting instruction from Divinity to enter the lifeform.

I saw a beautiful Light Being that gestured to a waiting soul, and then pointed downward toward Earth, 'You go there.' A life form was waiting there in utero, just waiting for a soul. The soul does in fact, experience the physical birth.

The important thing to remember is this: 'The soul is assigned with love, so that there is a continuation of life. The soul is assigned with love.' This has nothing to do with a specific moment during pregnancy, as it is a Divine decision, which is the essence of the mystery of life. There will never be a definitive answer in terms of the exact moment of a pregnancy when a soul is present, and we must accept this as the unanswered, sacred truth.

When I asked the Gift if we should add this into the book, and the answer I received is this, 'It is a teaching.' This teaching has many mysteries, and we, as humans, do not need to know everything. Whether that life is one minute long, or ninety-nine years long, that is the destiny of that soul in conjunction with that human life experience.

People wonder about how abortion fits into this equation. If it is the human's choice to terminate a pregnancy, what happens to the soul assigned by God? If God already knows the destiny of that fetus, and decides not to have a soul enter that womb? Or is that just a truly short 'life' that was only a blink of a human experience, in utero?

The answer I receive is this: God, the almighty Creator, assigns the soul to a life when God wants to, and then the human does whatever it desires during that life by exercising 'free will.' God will not, 'not assign' a soul based on the potential future outcome of the free will of another human being. Decisions such as these do affect one's karma since they are human actions that are the result of free will. The soul witnesses the action but does not judge. Judgement comes in the form of karma. Everything you do as a human affects your karma. If you do virtuous deeds, you are increasing your good karma. If you are doing terrible things, you are increasing your negative karma. Abortion is part of human behavior that does affect karma, as do all actions in a human lifetime. I asked the question, 'If an abortion occurs and a soul has already been assigned, what does that mean?' The answer I received is that it is a murder in a way, and that the soul experienced a 'death'. I was also shown that the act of abortion is much more humane at an earlier stage. I realize this is an upsetting and controversial discussion and ask you to look inside yourself deeply to find your own beliefs.

Erica wants to know if souls know each other. Do they travel in groups or cross paths? The answer I receive is that they do not necessarily have to have known each other prior to this human lifetime. Erica comments that some spiritual books discuss souls that can relate to one another in various space-times, and in one lifetime you can be a parent of a child and in another lifetime the two same souls can switch roles. The Gift tells me that there is a specific order to the interaction between souls, and there are groups of souls that travel together. They are assigned to people and families to create relationships. There are groupings who must work on all these relationships together on both a soul level and human life level. The souls must learn from one other and contribute to their collective growth and expansion toward total illumination. They may have had shared past life experiences. They could also go to other realms and travel without those souls in their group. There is infinite flexibility. It could be that in an incarnation a thousand years ago, some souls coexisted. Then, they completed other assignments before coming together again a thousand years later. Remember that these assignments are given with pure divine love.

Souls do recognize each other just like people, but when they come together again, they will have a fresh start. It is so unfathomably complex. The soul is part of the Divine, and if you have a connection between the human life and the soul, you understand your mission better. Healings don't always show me the person's soul, so many times, I see the human form only. The soul may be irrelevant to a healing if a physical or psychological illness relates to this current life and human issues only.

Soul Detachment

Sometimes, I see people with what I refer to as a "detached soul condition." These people are often depressed or emotionally distressed, yet unsure why. When I do this type of healing, I can often see that the soul is visibly disconnected from their body's form. There is no energetic connection from the soul to the body. I might see the soul and body side by side, showing me they aren't properly integrated as a unit. When there is a healthy connection, they coexist and overlap in a cohesive way.

I have witnessed this problem many times, which indicates to me that the journey of this soul requires more growth. The soul needs to be more nurtured and acknowledged during the person's human life and won't reintegrate with the human without the recognition it needs. It's almost as if the human behavior needs to rise to a higher, more positive level to meet with the soul, as the soul won't lower itself to meet the human at a less illuminated level. This issue is related to one's karma.

What is Karma?

Karma is a foreign concept in much of the Western world and particularly in the United States. As you perform selfless service in this lifetime, you essentially clean and clear your soul's karma. This has tremendous benefit to your soul in this life and in future incarnations. Your actions in this life benefit your soul in its next incarnation, which puts your soul in a better, higher position to embark on the next journey.

Human suffering is about karmic balance. It is a balancing tool within the realm of karma. The concept of karma is originally Hindu rather than Christian. Therefore, it is not fully adopted in America. The culture in India has much more of a thorough and longstanding cultural understanding of karma. But if you do deeds that serve others without an expectation of reward or recognition, it will help your soul's journey whether you recognize the concept of karma or not. That said, I believe it's better to be aware of the concept of karma. It certainly is not the only reason people choose to do good things, but it's a powerful incentive.

In the type of healing where I see soul detachment, I must explain what I was shown in a delicate and kind way. I talk to the person about recognizing that their soul is part of them, what it needs, and what they can do to feel connected to their soul. A healing can often tell me specifically what a person needs to do to bring about this alignment. Taking positive action will help to integrate soul and body. Maybe the soul needs more or is expecting more out of this human life? The soul has a process rooted in its own development and is much more advanced than the human. So, as I said, the person must raise their level of goodness to meet the soul on its higher level.

Erica asked me about depression, wanting to know if it's tied to the well-known spiritual concept of the "Dark Night of the Soul." I asked, and The Gift tells me it is a form of "Spiritual Blindness." It is a time when the soul isn't able to assist a person's growth. The soul is stuck. Souls are energy, you see, but they are also beings that exist with a path to follow, and individuality based on their history of existences. Knowledge, enrichment, experience, and the number of reincarnations make each soul unique.

"Old" and "New" Souls

I can intuitively perceive when someone is an old soul. By "old soul," I mean someone who has been here on earth before. I believe that at some point, when the soul has done its required work, it doesn't need to experience more earthly lifetimes.

"Old" versus "new" is not the best description for a soul, however. The phrase "old soul" refers more accurately to a "wise" soul. It is not actually about age or time, but about the amount and quality of experiences. Since existence is all about growth and expansion, a soul with innumerable incarnations may not actually be an "old" soul in terms of wisdom.

Once, while performing a healing on a young man, I saw that his soul was reaching upward and climbing out of the earth. It was an extraordinary scene unlike any I'd ever experienced. I perceived that his was a new soul being born from the earth into its very first incarnation, and his soul was emerging from a worm or perhaps the earth itself.

After the healing, his friends said he was constantly hugging trees! He is a free spirit who lives with no physical home and almost no possessions.

Imagine that souls are like leaves that have fallen from trees. You see a meandering stream and a tree beside it, and a leaf falls from the tree and floats downstream in the water. There's another leaf floating down the stream that fell into the water earlier, further upstream. This leaf has been floating down the stream for some time. Eventually, the two leaves join and float together down the same stretch of stream. One leaf has more experience in the river, while the other has newly fallen into the water. But they journey together.

Soul Connections

Erica questioned me about arrangements and connections between souls. She told me a college friend of hers, Mike, suddenly passed away recently. "DK, also my dear friend," she said, "was devastated by the loss. DK told me that he had suffered so many tragic deaths in his life and didn't know why he had to experience so much loss. His older brother died of leukemia, and another friend died in his arms after a suicide attempt. Was there a soul arrangement between these brothers and friends?"

I told her that I do not know the purpose of these arrangements, but I passionately believe there is one. There are many situations and relationships between souls that are intertwined. The complexity of soul connections is truly astounding. The healing of Laura illuminates this complexity further, later in this chapter.

So, you could be living today with another human being and your souls may have shared a past life experience. You are not aware of it as a human, although some people say they can sense this. They are assigned from pools of souls to a more specific, smaller group, and from there they are assigned a mission, or life. They also could go to other realms and travel without those souls in their group. Things are not on a 'set' path, and there is infinite flexibility. They can travel together but do not always. Remember the time of the soul and the time on Earth is completely different. It could be that in an incarnation a thousand years ago souls co-existed, then they had other assignments and a thousand years later, they are together again during another lifetime. There is a reason for the assignments. Remember: 'Assigned in love.'

The soul is part of the Divine and if you have a connection between the human life and the soul, you understand your mission better. The soul may be irrelevant to a healing if the healing is for the physical body only. A physical or psychological illness may need to be healed in this current life situation, period. A healing for today, with human issues in this lifetime, is the most straightforward type of healing I do.

The Healing of Laura and her Egyptian past life.

While getting a treatment at a surgeon's office, Erica met Laura, who worked there as a nurse. She told Erica she had suffered from lifelong feelings of deep loneliness. It was a heavy burden that she could not easily describe. She thought it might be related to her recent divorce, but then she recalled that she had these negative feelings as far back as her childhood. Laura sent me a photo of herself with her two small children. She had concerns that her husband and his mother would impact the health and happiness of the kids. She wondered if there was some sort of spiritual aspects to the difficulties in the relationship.

When I began the healing, however, I didn't see anything related to her husband and his family or her children. The first vision I received was a dark room with a massive rectangular grey stone in the center with the figure of a black dog perched on top of it. The dog was lying down with his paws in front of him, and he had pointed ears and a very pointy snout. He appeared very formal and official. The stone was large and as tall as my chest.

I was instructed by the Gift to move the stone, but I didn't know why. I leaned against it in my mind's eye with as much leverage as I could gather, and the heavy stone would not move. I then slid my hands up to the corner of the stone and pushed again. The stone was a box! The top of the box slid over slightly about four or five inches. The moment the box was opened just a sliver, a luminous, multi-colored thing came out of it fast like a comet, zooming past me directly upward. The colors were mostly red, yellow, and white, and it was a narrow flash like a laser light. I knew it was a release of some sort, and I sensed it was trapped souls. To prevent them from being trapped again, I pushed the top of the box over until it fell onto the ground. The Gift told me that Laura's soul had witnessed the opening of the box and the release of the trapped souls. She had not been trapped herself, but these souls had been her friends. Her soul had been waiting for these other souls to be released, all the while suffering with the knowing that they had been trapped for so long. This manifested as her feelings of loneliness in this lifetime.

I spoke to Laura again after a few days, and she told me she no longer felt the anguish and sadness. Her face on the video was glowing and luminous. I did another healing on her a few weeks later and saw her soul like a ballet dancer leaping in a field of flowers with butterflies. I saw her as a complete human and soul combination, touching flowers and dressed in a beautiful white dress. She was filled with joy. Her pain was the result of seeing the suffering of others. Since they were freed, so was she.

Before this healing, I didn't know souls could be trapped in this way. I was told that they were trapped as a punishment by enormously powerful forces but not specifically dark forces. Souls are Divine, so they can't be possessed. I don't know anything more than that about this phenomenon, and I think it's best not to analyze it too much. I only know what I saw, and I could be wrong about why this happened to these souls. For me, the focus was on Laura's healing.

Interestingly, after setting up the first Zoom session for me with Laura, on the same day, Erica randomly took her children to the Egyptian section of the Metropolitan Museum of Art in New York City. She stopped in front of a sarcophagus with the figure of Anubis the dog sitting on top. She examined the details of the box, including the eyes carved into the side. After I shared the details of Laura's healing, Erica wanted to know if the sarcophagus I saw in my vision was currently in New York. But the Gift told me, "There are many copies. Not a relevant question." So, the "coincidence" here is a mystery.

Testimony of Laura: The Healing of her Egyptian past life.

Before my healing, I had an overwhelming feeling of heaviness that I carried with me. I couldn't put my finger on what it was but there was a sadness that felt deep. I had had a few years of hardships so I'm sure they were contributing but I felt like there was something standing in between me being able to heal or recover. It was preventing me from moving forward, I felt I was stuck in a quicksand of emotions. Despite my hardships, there was just something else there. I met Erica and she talked to me about Angel, she completely had no idea I had been feeling the way I was. No one would because it did not show on the surface. It was a struggle that only I faced on my own, privately.

I immediately set myself up to chat with Angel. It was very emotional for me. Upon meeting him on zoom I felt suddenly emotional, which is uncommon for me. He told me what he saw -a dark object like a basket or barrel. Something that would hold something. When he got closer and etherically moved the object, from the object a blast of light scattered upward.

Angel gave me some tools. He asked me to ask my Light to protect me and my family. He told me to stand in the sunlight, close my eyes and imagine the light acting as a blanket. 'Allow the light to come over me, feel it cover my head, then shoulders then down my body.' It was such an emotional and spiritual moment.

As the days passed and weeks, I felt free. Lighter. It's been about one year, and I couldn't feel better. I feel like I let go of something that was holding me down. I feel grateful and I continue to ask the Light to protect me and my children.

The Healing of the WWII Soldier

One day when I was working at the Olive Leaf wellness center in New York City, there was a thin, funny guy in his mid-thirties who came into the waiting room and said, "I will only see you if you tell me the color of my dog." "I'm not interested in telling you the color of your dog," I responded. "If you want to come for a healing, you should." The following week, he decided to do it.

As the healing began, I saw a graphic scene of war. A soldier with a machine gun shot another soldier at point blank range. I told him what was shown to me, and he asked which war it was. I went back into the vision and saw that the shooter wore a World War II German helmet, and he shot a British soldier. The man then told me that his body was no longer functioning. His organs were apparently failing, and doctors had told him that if he got sick again, he would probably die. Somehow, I understood that his soul was carrying the physical pain of the soldier who had been shot. He then disclosed that his great-grandfather, who was British, had been killed in combat in WWII. His body was ravaged from that shooting. This man was carrying the pain of his own ancestor.

This sort of pain is often seen in family constellations with transference of ancestral issues from family members on different timelines. The influence of past family members into the life of someone today can be quite pronounced. If a past family member was murdered or raped, someone in the future might unconsciously take on that suffering, and it can affect them in an intense way physically or emotionally. This doesn't mean that the man and his great-grandfather shared the same soul. There's a fundamental connection that isn't the physical body between those two men. The only other connection would be through the soul, but I'm not sure how or why this occurs. An immensely powerful Being of Light told me, "It is Divine," meaning that the connection between them is Divine. And Divine may mean that the memory is transferred somehow through Divinity. There are certain concepts that we, as humans, aren't capable of comprehending.

Dr. Bert Hellinger was a German Jesuit priest who, after leaving the priesthood, became a psychotherapist and developed the groundbreaking method of 'Family Constellations'. Ron Young, the healer, and my root teacher, works very well in this modality. Hellinger's books are technical and complex because he looks at all behaviors happening within a family. In a family constellation, there is one person who desires healing. During the constellation people are chosen as placeholders to represent the person's family members, so their family does not necessarily have to be present (or willing) as participants. The constellator must be adept and able to open to the 'scene' that unfolds and facilitate the movements.

The book <u>The Ancestor Syndrome by Anne Ancelin Schutzenberger</u> is fascinating. People that are participating as placeholders for family members take on the personalities of the assigned member and act out the family dynamic. The constellator analyzes the scene and how the members interacted. There can be a lot of pain and anger and fighting, but no one gets physically injured. I remember being in Italy witnessing a family constellation where Cathy was chosen to take on a role. Another participant was a huge former wrestling Olympian. In the constellation Cathy started fighting with him, hitting him over and over, he would grab her arms, but he did not hurt her. It was very frightening for me to witness since he could have knocked her out with one blow. I know there is tremendous healing in constellation work, but this modality of healing is not revealed to me. It is important to know that influences of past lives could affect a person's current life.

Erica looked into her family history and tree online and was able to go back to the 1500s in Sweden. There were some Swedish ancestors who gave birth up to forty times with only a few babies surviving into adulthood. Erica feels like it would be a tremendous amount of pain and loss to carry and potentially transfer through the generations when as far back as great-great grandparents can affect your experience today. Erica wonders why children can have such different personalities. Is it genetic? What is a personality? Where does it come from?

I believe an individual's personality is a combination of traits that come from their genetics, their environment, and their spiritual history. Family constellations can help resolve personality issues today that result from events that occurred as far back as seven generations. Family constellations work to heal the suffering and patterns that have been transferred down through generations. The constellator must have the ability to understand the intricacies of the lives, how they are intertwined, and know when there is a satisfactory resolution. It is a complex and highly effective healing modality. Family can be such a source of suffering and growth for so many people.

Final Words on the Soul

Do souls choose what life they want to experience? I have understood that the soul does what it's told by the highest power of God. I have seen that there is a hierarchy within Divinity, and the souls are part of this hierarchy. If the soul made its own decision, it would be like a soldier deciding what he wants to do on his own in a battle. It's the magnificent and complex cycle of karmic repair, growth, and expansion. And some souls do not come here at all. They go to other places in the cosmos about which we don't know.

Of course, the soul is here to grow and learn, and our notion of time is a human construct that doesn't necessarily align with a soul's journey. You could have an uneventful life, but at one miraculous point, there will be an opening in your awareness that expands you spiritually. As human beings, it's impossible for us to fathom the full and true grandeur of the soul's journey toward illumination.

Do Animals Have Souls?

Animals have souls, but it's a different type. They have a "being of energy" that has a lesser level of intensity than the human soul. Human beings are an essential part of all creation created by Divinity itself. Therefore, they're directly connected to the Divine, and our souls look very particular to me. I don't see the same thing when I look at animals. I see something that seems to be in a more primitive stage of development that isn't fully formed or as powerful.

6 OBSERVING BUFO CEREMONIES

(Disclaimer: Nothing contained in this book is intended to encourage the use of illegal substances. Using psychedelics is not without risk. Psychedelics can potentially produce extremely uncomfortable, frightening, confusing, painful, and physically and psychologically destabilizing experiences. We do not recommend using Bufo.)

When a man named Juan was referred to me for a healing, he told me he performs his own type of healings on people using a substance called "Bufo." Juan is an American psychiatrist who grew weary of seeing his patients unable to resolve their suffering. So, he decided to explore indigenous shamanic healing methods. He was trained to administer Bufo by a native Mexican who is experienced in its use.

Juan proposed exchanging healing experiences, and I agreed. I worked on Juan first so that my mind was clear and unaffected by the Bufo. Then, shortly after, I began my own Bufo experience. I wasn't seeking any particular outcome other than to explore the modality, which at that time I didn't consider as "healing."

What exactly is a Bufo ceremony? The substance is a venom that is extracted from the Bufo Alvarius toad and then crystalized. It's scientifically referred to as 5-MeO-DMT, an extremely potent psychedelic. During a ceremony, an exceedingly small amount of the substance is inhaled from a pipe, giving the person an instantly powerful hallucinogenic experience. I have observed that for a ten-minute period, the individual travels somewhere else spiritually. The total Bufo ceremony process lasts about 30 to 45 minutes.

The Bufo treatment concept is to "release the ego" and clean spiritual blockages. People say they feel much better afterwards, and the belief is that Bufo can help with anxiety, post-traumatic stress disorder, depression, and other mental health issues.

During the healing I performed on Juan, I immediately saw the Hindu god Ganesh standing behind him. Ganesh's arms were outstretched around him while he administered the Bufo. I innately understood that Ganesh was performing the ceremony through Juan. I was astonished to see Ganesh since Juan isn't Hindu and hasn't been to India. Having travelled to India three times myself, I was familiar with the elephant-human depiction of this god who represents the remover of obstacles. Juan was also surprised but pleased that Ganesh appeared as his Bufo guide.

My own Bufo healing was a non-event in that I didn't experience any visions or unusual feelings. Sometime afterwards, however, I was able to expand my healing ability. If a person asked me a question, I could ask that question and direct the healing to receive an answer. This newfound flexibility enhanced my healing ability considerably. I cannot be sure, of course, that Bufo had anything to do with that expansion. While I observed others as they experienced Bufo, I could specifically see the position of their souls in relation to an area where Divine Beings were gathered. I could see the obstacles and the beauty of their soul's connection to that Divinity.

Since then, I have traveled to see these ceremonies in various locations. To date, I've witnessed roughly 100 Bufo healings. I often share my perceptions with the members of Juan's healing group, and I perform individual healings on people who wish to hear my observations of their Bufo experience.

My Visions While Observing Bufo Ceremonies

Few people can recall the details of what happened during the five to ten minutes right after inhaling the frog venom smoke. Some people lay quietly, and some react with spitting bile, yelling, and thrashing around. Others verbally express their amazement at their hallucinations. Juan and his assistant are there to settle and calm those who react physically. I have learned, however, that the person's physical reaction has nothing to do with the images of their soul that I see during the healing.

The part that interests me is from the moment of inhalation for roughly ten minutes. During that initial ten minutes, I consistently see the same scenario unfold. The moment a person inhales the crystallized venom through a pipe, they collapse from a sitting position. They are "gone" for those ten minutes. Then, for about 20 minutes, they move toward reintegrating themselves. The significant part of my observation begins at the moment of inhalation. After my viewing, I walk away to record my vision, and I return when they're recovering.

The healing vision I see is a sequence of revealing images that show the position of the soul in this incarnation in relation to the Divine Beings in what I refer to as the Kingdom of Ganesh. After viewing so many ceremonies, I have come to understand the overall vision in its entirety. I see the soul as an elongated shape of glowing light without much detail. It's always on a path trying to move toward a dark grey platform. Sometimes, there are obstacles along the pathway, and the soul can't advance to the platform. These blockages need to be removed so that the soul can continue to the platform.

I have worked with people after their Bufo sessions to remove those obstacles, and in subsequent Bufo sessions, their souls have been able to proceed further. Whenever a soul arrives at the platform, it appears to look upward. Some stay in that position, while others start to rise. As the soul ascends, the surrounding area becomes more luminous and lighter grey. At some point during that ascension, the soul stops moving upward and remains hovering from side to side at that level, looking upward but unable to continue the ascent. I have come to understand that at this point, they have reached the level where they are in this incarnation. The higher the soul ascends, the brighter the surrounding light. Some souls eventually end up remarkably close to or within the tiered, arched amphitheater where Ganesh is at the top in the middle of the arch, surrounded by other Divine Beings below him to his right and left.

Prior to one ceremony, we were gathered in a garden with a table covered with stones, crystals, and other objects. I randomly picked up a piece of wood to examine it, but I felt nothing. It was from the Ayahuasca tree. Someone told me the root is boiled, and other elements are added in a specific recipe to create the tea. I then reached for a tiny bowl with a few crystals of Bufo in it, sat down, and balanced the bowl on my thigh as I examined it. I immediately started going upward spiritually, without even ingesting it. I was elevating just by holding the tiny bowl! It showed me the power of this venom. Another time, however, I felt absolutely nothing when I rested a bowl of Bufo on my thigh. Juan told me that the one I had held the previous day was already energized with spiritual intention through ceremony.

I once witnessed another person administering Bufo in a more mechanical and business-like way. The session was less spiritual in nature, and I didn't observe the presence of Ganesh or the platform. People are also now using a man-made chemical compound version. I haven't observed people using this artificial substance but am interested to see if Ganesh is present there as well. There are a few cases of people who can recall what happened to them under Bufo, including what they felt during those moments of soul ascension. I always suggest to people taking it that they try to recall their experience as soon as they start to come out of the effect. It's like trying to remember a dream that will fade quickly.

In one Bufo session, I saw a Divine Being appear to witness and oversee a woman's ceremony and ascension. I asked who he was, and the answer was "Sumerian, Assyrian from Mesopotamia." This soul was not just any soul; it was a soul that had been significant in his kingdom. That was the only time I observed a being from another realm of time-space reality enter the ceremony. How many more dimensions are there? The complexity I see is enormous.

Bufo Ceremony of a Young Woman as a Goddess

One Bufo ceremony I observed was particularly fantastic. The young woman's spirit sat with the Divine Beings in the amphitheater. At first, I saw a bright red light as she ascended directly to the lower left side of the amphitheater. There were less important Divine Beings at that height of the arch, and they indicated that they couldn't alter their position. They welcomed her and proceeded to show her their power and the expansive world below them—an entire luminous universe.

After she had a second dose of Bufo, she was in the amphitheater again. The Divine Beings were all illuminated, and she was one of them. It was very bright and beautiful, and a figure that I knew to be the All Powerful came down to Ganesh, who was seated at the top in the center. This 'All Powerful being' kissed Ganesh on the head.

When the girl was recovering from her Bufo experience, I made sure I was right there to encourage her to go back in her mind to see if she could recall what she experienced. Without any knowledge of what I had seen, she said she went home where she was a Goddess. This was exactly what I had recorded minutes earlier.

Below is a transcript of some of our conversation:

Angel: What happened at the beginning?

Woman: It felt like home, really.

Angel: Where is home?

Woman: In here, in myself. My true self.

Angel: Out of what? Go deeper. You must go deeper.

Woman: I was out of my ego; I had no ego. But I felt like something I have always been. Like the truth. What I have always been.

Angel: What have you always been? Let go and go deeper.

Woman: Like truth. The person that came to mind was like, me—a healer?

Angel: It is more than that.

Woman: I don't want to say what I'm thinking—a Goddess or something. Yes, I was a Goddess.
Angel: Yes, you were a Goddess. Where, tell me?

Woman: It is something I have always known.

Angel: Yes. It was revealed to you.

Woman: I don't know where I was—some sort of heaven.
Angel: What were you shown when you were there?

Woman: Everything. The whole kingdom. It was so beautiful. It doesn't seem real, but it is. [She began to cry.]

Angel: You're telling me what I saw. Absolutely.

Woman: Wow, wow, wow!

Angel: You were right there, not to the top, but right near there. It was a direct flight, and then you were shown the kingdom. The second trip, you beautifully illuminated all the Gods of your specific level. You were in one level of Divine Beings, and there were levels above you. It was a beautiful thing. You are an old soul. What you told me is exactly what I saw, and this is something that you now will always carry with you and think about because you are much wiser than you think you are. And you are a Goddess.

The woman was twenty-five years old and completely shocked and overwhelmed by this knowledge. Before this session, she shared with me that she was changing and evolving, as she was becoming a vegetarian and reading about India. I feel that this knowledge will absolutely change her trajectory in a profound way. Her spiritual journey had begun in this life. It was an amazing session for me as well because I saw more than usual. She was an "old," experienced soul and a Goddess in another realm, and now, she is experiencing a human life.

Ally's Bufo Ceremony

Ally, who is Juan's assistant, also had a fascinating Bufo session in which I saw her as the Goddess Shiva, filled with her own bright white light. I saw Ganesh descend from above to join her soul on the platform. I had never witnessed this before. Ganesh then proceeded to ascend with Shiva/Ally into the amphitheater of the Gods. In

Hinduism, Shiva is the divine father of Ganesh. I witnessed their beautiful trip together upward.

Delving Deeper into the frog and Ganesh

Interestingly, when Erica asked me to question the Gift as to whether the Bufo venom is connected to Hinduism, I first did not get an answer. When I asked again, I received the answer that Ganesh does not want to be associated with the frog. He wants to be a part of this only when the soul trip occurs. Ganesh witnesses soul ascensions and is too powerful to be connected to the earthly frog. The venom is just a tool with no innate spiritual power. It alters the human physiology to allow for the experience but is not holy or part of Divinity.

Erica intuitively feels that I have some sort of connection to India and the Hindu religion. Maybe a significant past life experience in India? She would like me to ask the Gift about my connection to the Hindu religion. Erica believes the connection is through me and not the actual frog, which incidentally is from the Sonoran Desert in Mexico. The answer is that spiritually I had been in India a long time ago. I saw a vision of Amma in India, and I saw that I was a spirit there in India. Erica knows that my soul journey has a part that happened in India and the frog itself is not connected to India, but I am on a soul level and that India could be my root soul's birthplace.

The frog venom is merely the vehicle. Erica reminds me that Amma did say, 'Your trip to India started a long time ago.' She knew you had already been there, and she told you. (See Chapter on India.) Erica is thrilled that the Gift just confirmed that I was spiritually in India a long time ago. I am constantly surprised by my Gift. I thought the Bufo itself was connected to Ganesh, and that I was only observing their connection. What we have discovered just now is completely different set of circumstances!

Erica would like to explore this topic further and would like me to ask this important question: When your soul's time was in India what was your role? Who were you? What did you do there? The answer I receive is in the form of images. I witnessed a young man with Indian features, walking very calmly wearing a white robe. He exists in total peace. Very relaxed. He speaks to others in a very calm manner. I see a very humble area in rural India. He is talking to many people. He is wise. He was then attacked and killed by the people that did not believe him. They threw stones at him.

Erica wonders if I somehow witnessed a miniscule piece of the Christ energy in a past life. I do know that Christ lived many years in India, from the time he was sixteen to about thirty-two years old, he travelled in India. There are books written about it and his robes were from Indian sewing techniques in the Indian manner. There is a saint named Issa which many believe was in fact, Jesus.

Erica's theory is that the essence of Christ is shared throughout humanity if we are quiet and faithful enough to receive it. His entire essence is transmitted through many souls, and to disperse this massive energy, God spreads the power amongst his divine creation: human beings. So, someone else may feel a connection to that same energy source, and recall a time spent in Bethlehem in a barn with animals and family, and feel a deep, transcendent peace. What a beautiful conversation. We sat in silence awhile.

Erica inquires as to her connection with the book and with me. She feels that we knew each other in another lifetime. When I ask the Gift if we knew each before this life, the answer I receive is that she has listened to me in the past. Erica's response was an emphatic, 'I knew it!' Erica asked if she was there with me in India. The answer is yes. There are so many complexities that we do not understand.

Erica shared that when we spoke about Amma she felt an intense, enveloping feeling of love that surrounded her for days. She literally felt love emanating in a sphere of about ten feet that surrounded her. It was a surreal experience. There is something about India.

In all seriousness, we must remember we are discussing ethereal topics. We are trying to understand the existence and complexity of the spiritual world from our limited perspective. This is the journey of the soul. Each journey heads home to same place but each soul has a wildly experience.

7 EXORCISMS, EVIL, AND EGO

Sometimes, I immediately see bad or dark energies attached to people, and I know I must work to free the person from those energies. These healings are presented to me from a higher power, and I perform my work with my highest respect and focus.

I always see these energies in the color black and as giant, hideous insects or wild dog-like creatures such as hyenas. I refer to them as "monsters" or sometimes "demons." I believe that we are naturally protected, but sometimes, negative energies can penetrate our natural luminous energy field. These dark entities attach to humans in a parasitic way, and their purpose is to cause suffering.

The monsters have different levels of strength. They attack me during my work to exorcise them, but I have always been able to defend myself. I know God is present with me in these situations, so I don't fear the attacks. Some of these healings are more intense than others but I know that with the help of God I will be able to handle them. I have never had any expectation of what I am going to see or what will happen when a healing ensues because trying to figure out what will happen is irrelevant to me and not helpful. I consider an exorcism as a removal of monsters, and there is a difference between having a monster 'on' a person or 'near' a person. It is easier to perform the healing when the negative energies are less powerful and not attached to a person's body. Why are the monsters there? These dark entities need to attach to humans in a parasitic way, and their purpose is to cause suffering.

I force the monsters away and separate them from the person with Divine Light emanating through my hands. I direct the Light at them, which they hate. They usually come back two or three times, sometime attacking me viciously. I must defend myself. With the Light, I'm eventually able to force them to lay prostrate at the base of the cross of Jesus as a priest once told me to do. The cross of Jesus is always present in an exorcism. I force them to the cross to prostrate in front of God. I don't send them anywhere else, and I can't destroy or convert them. I can't transform something evil into something good. Remember, these monsters have an essence, and they are elementals; meaning that they do exist.

Few Spiritual Healings require an exorcism. When they do, I see the human form in front of me with the monsters around the body, sometimes grabbing onto or biting the body as if inflicting pain. Sometimes, the monsters don't want me to see them, so they attempt to hide and cower behind the person. It's important to clarify that I see these monsters attached to the human body, not the soul. They can't attach to the soul, as it's pure Divinity and bright light.

When I see that someone is possessed, I tell them about the existence of good and bad energies and explain that what's happening to them isn't unusual. I refer to them as "light exorcisms" so that people aren't scared by the words, "exorcism" and "possessed." I want to avoid the terrifying imagery of movies like The Exorcist.

I explain that I will work with Spiritual Light to rid them of these disturbing energies. When I start an exorcism, as with all my healings, I ask God to help me. I then proceed to focus on the monsters and push them away from the person with Spiritual Light that comes from my Being of Light, as well as the Being of Light of the person receiving the healing. Some of these energies refuse to leave and move toward me as if attacking me. In the order of evil, the more powerful demons are more aggressive. I have seen three, four, or five on one person simultaneously.

Once the monsters/demons are gone, I create what I call a "Cupola of Light" around the person as protection. The monsters can't come back near the person for a short period of time, if ever. The individual must regularly protect themself with Divine Light, as the energies will linger around someone like a hungry dog. They will go away eventually, however, if not fed. As I mentioned, I teach people to do this Light work so that they can continue protecting themselves for at least a week. They must ask their Being of Light to send them Divine Light.

When my wife Cathy and I had dinner with a couple in Argentina many years ago, the woman we were dining with knew I was a Spiritual Healer and suggested I contact a priest in Buenos Aires who performed Catholic exorcisms. I was intrigued to hear his thoughts, so I called him the next morning to introduce myself and explain what I did. His angry response was startling. "Who authorized you to do these? Have you been authorized by the Pope? Did you go to the Congress of Exorcists in Mexico last year?" I told him I once met a Catholic priest who gave me a method to follow. "The priest was wrong to give you this! He should never have given you any information!" he screamed back at me. "You shouldn't do this. We take this seriously! When we suspect someone needs an exorcism, we suggest one year of psychotherapy, and then, we determine if an exorcism is in fact needed."

"Do you see the monsters?" I asked. "No, I don't." "Well, I see them immediately. I can tell if someone is possessed in two seconds." "I don't want to continue this conversation!" he yelled and hung up. After seeing those dark energies once, twice, fifty, one hundred times, why am I going to doubt their existence in our world? I don't doubt their existence, and I do what the Gift guides me to do in order to help those that are suffering from evil energies.

Healing Possessed People

Healing of the Troubled Man in Argentina

For some time, I worked with a group of mental health professionals in Buenos Aires. There was a patient who screamed at us and became physically aggressive during his first visit. It was a terrible scene. When he returned the following week, he came close to attacking one of the psychiatrists.

Prior to the third week's visit, I told the other doctors that I thought the man was fully possessed. I suggested to them that I be present in the room but separated from the others. My plan was to work on releasing him from his monsters. Throughout the session, as I released the energies from him, he didn't raise his voice and was transformed into the calmest person you could imagine. The doctors were shocked by the transformation. During the man's fourth visit, I closed my eyes occasionally to make sure the energies hadn't reattached to him.

What does it mean to be "fully" possessed? I define it as being overrun by too many demons. The man reacted in an overly aggressive way because these monsters were all around him, constantly attacking him. The more aggressive they are, the more evil they are. In some instances, they're weak, and I see them as small and less aggressive.

It's especially sad when a child is possessed. Children of today suffer from many behavioral illnesses, and in my experience, it's sometimes the result of possession, which can greatly affect their behavior and moods.

The Healing of Tomas

A woman named Dolores brought me her four-year-old child named Tomas. "He doesn't speak," she told me, "but he's affectionate." When I saw him, I immediately perceived the negative energies attached to his back. I began to walk around him, attempting to look at his back. He squirmed in his seat to try to hide his back from me. The monster was making him move to remain hidden from me. Dolores described Tomas further in this way: "He was disinterested in things, few smiles, few words, and avoided eye contact. His diagnosis was mild ASD (autism spectrum disorder)."

I would never say to a parent, "your child is possessed." I use phrases like "disturbing energies" and teach the parents how to work with Divine Light to protect their child. I worked on the boy to separate the monster from him, and his mother continued the work by covering him with Divine Light every day. Two weeks after the healing, the boy began to speak. I understand that after a few months, he changed schools and is living a normal life.

Testimony of Tomas' Mother, Dolores.

I am Dolores, the mother of Tomas. I desperately wanted to help my son when I contacted Ángel, I did not know who or what I would encounter. At that time, Tomas was a child that was 'not happy' (not sad, I do not identify him with that word), he was disinterested in things, few smiles, few words, and he avoided eye contact…. his diagnosis was ASD (autism spectrum disorder), fortunately, in this case, mild. However, beyond how traditional medicine was helping us and what we were being told, we were missing something, or someone: Angel.

The first meeting was difficult for me; I had to leave the aura of my beloved son in the hands of a stranger. My son avoided Angel and hid from him. The tranquility and peace in the environment managed to calm him, and Angel was able to do what he knows: to help, to take away the darkness that, for reasons unknown to us, had occupied the world of my son.

Angel explained to me what he saw, and what he had been able to do. He gave me 'homework', which I diligently completed, not only because I needed to do everything I possibly could, but also because of the conviction of my belief and the peace that Angel had transmitted to me. When I saw Angel, I left with a sense of tranquility that did not correspond to my mood at the time. And from then on…a few days passed and that 'not happy' expression of Tomy's began to transform. All that Light, all that protection that Tomy was receiving was bearing fruit. He became an interested and connected child, and most of all HAPPY. He left behind his rages and frustrations. He became receptive to conventional therapies, and we continue to always protect him with Light… Light… Light.

Healing of the California Boy

I also had a unique case with a young boy in California, who knows he's possessed, as does his mother. The monsters talk to him, and he talks to them. I've been working with him regularly, but remotely. I can see the monsters around him from long distance. I actually wish he would call me twenty times a day so that we could rid him of the monsters.

Whenever we meet, he starts the session by growling at me. He told me recently that there's an evil soldier-monster, black and blue with shining red eyes, who tells him that he must fulfill his destiny. Where does that idea come from? Who is that monster? It is a demon. He told me that he sees it, and then he glares at me with a monstrous expression. He then says he only saw the monster one time and tries to downplay it. I saw that same demon that he described attached to him. We both saw the same thing.

"What is your destiny?" I asked. "Money laundering and robbing people."

I haven't yet been able to remove the monster from him. Two issues are that we're working remotely, and there's no continuity to our sessions. He calls me randomly whenever he wants. I've told him to call me anytime, and I've taught him to work with his Being of Light. I ask him regularly if he's doing the work, but it doesn't appear he is. It's a sad situation, but again, people have to want to heal. You see, negative energies do exist in our world, and we must do our best to avoid connecting to them. However, it is not unusual to find people who consciously connect to evil energies with the desire to hurt others.

If there is someone that hates you, wants to hurt you, and they have access to evil, they can hurl energy for your destruction. This can affect you and no one else. This possession originates from one person sending a monster to attack and inflict pain on a person of their choosing. There are humans with evil powers who can direct bad energy to negatively affect you and hurt you.

In a way, the sender is also possessed, but by the 'whole entity of evil'. In another instance in Argentina, while performing a healing on a young boy, I was unable to release him from an aggressive and powerful monster. I called my friend Ron Young and asked for his assistance. He recommended that we bring in a healer from Nigeria, whom I'd met in New York. He suggested some rituals that we performed together with the parents, but we had to continue with more intensity to remove the evil attachment. The parents decided they didn't want to continue because the rituals required were too "out there" for them.

In Nigeria, powerful rituals have been used for generations.

Healing of the Musician with the Black Flies

We once did a healing on an Italian musician who had travelled to Nigeria to work. Upon return, he was suffering from apparent cancer. His entire band had been energetically attacked while there. When he first came in to work with our group in Italy, he was very arrogant, and the monster was extremely aggressive. He had an enormous monster, and when our group put our hands on him, hundreds of black flies entered through the open windows and began covering our hands and arms. We had actual flies all over us!

He came three days in a row for us to work on him. By the third day, he was crying from gratitude, as he felt so much better. He could feel the relief. The Nigerian's ancient traditions are highly powerful, and they can control entities. This music group had been cursed in Nigeria and now, sadly, the entire band is dead.

Exorcisms that include Pain Inflicted by Other Human Beings

There are also people who consciously connect to evil energies with the desire to hurt others. This was the case with Erica's friend, Pat.

The Healing of the Woman with Parental Anguish

As I began Pat's healing, I saw a giant, grotesque hyena-like monster eating her alive. This evil monster was different from the usual ones I see because it was sent deliberately to devour her. It was particularly aggressive. I don't recall seeing another one so vividly, which made me think that although the creature was coming from the same origin of evil, it was infinitely more dangerous.

This type of monster can move freely and not remain attached to a specific human, but it has a purpose. It was specifically sent to this person to attack her by someone who wanted to inflict severe emotional pain on her. This type of attack creates tremendous internal suffering. "Does somebody hate you?" I asked Pat.

When she answered "yes," I asked her to show me a picture of the person. The moment before she showed me the photo, I knew exactly who it was. I perceived two people: her father and mother. Her parents have direct access to evil, which would give them the capacity to send this creature at their will to whomever they choose. My guess is that they probably didn't comprehend exactly what they were doing in terms of how much bad energy they were activating and what it was doing to their daughter. But they both had the innate desire to inflict pain on her. The father, who is now dead, put it in motion well beforehand. He may have been separated from his soul when he was living. (We'll discuss the phenomenon of Soul Separation in a later chapter.)

The monster remained on its mission even after the father died. I suspect her dad was much more powerful than her mother. My impression was that they weren't possessed by evil but embodied evil, which I find to be quite rare. This healing involved a human being that wanted to destroy another, their own child. Tragic.

During Pat's healing, I perceived the energy of her father near the monster. I was able to send him away with a wave of Light. Then, I had to detach the monster that was devouring her. Although it attacked me, I focused strongly with Light on defending myself and succeeded in sending it to the foot of the cross of Jesus. I then taught her to protect herself under the Cupola of Light.

At the time of her healing, she showed me photographs of her three children. I perceived that two of them had serious issues and were suffering. They had witnessed the anguish of their mother and needed protection. So, after her healing, I worked with the rest of her family. None of the others were possessed, but I taught them all how to protect themselves with Light.

Helping this family filled me with such joy, and they were so appreciative. Pat must be protected with Light before she sees her mother so that her energy field can't be invaded. She can learn to change the pattern of her relationship with her mother that's been in place for 50 years, but it won't happen overnight. She can't lower her guard. A year later, however, Pat's life had been transformed. Her face visibly changed into a content and smiling expression. She moved into a new house in a new city. Her children looked happy, bright, and emotionally connected to the world around them. She continued to practice the Cupola of Light protection around herself and her family. It has been a gift for Erica to witness this change in her friend.

Pat explains that her family had "experienced years of family trauma where darkness had come over me and my children. For a period of three years, it felt as if there was no joy or lightness around our family. I went to Angel, thinking the healing was for my son, but as he started working with the Light and healing him, he encountered that there were specific demons and dark forces around me trying to cause me and my family harm. After that session, I felt a real shift. Since the healings, we're moving forward and onward. The energy of each one of us has been profoundly changed. I'm deeply grateful to Angel and to Erica for making the introduction and giving me the courage to seek him out."

Erica subsequently asked me what happens if someone make decisions that inadvertently inflict pain on members of their family or others rather than on purpose as in the case of Pat's parents. The intention is most important, as well as the efforts to make amends. Of course, at times, we may need to remove ourselves from a situation to self-protect, even though it could hurt others and cause them pain. But our intent in that instance isn't to inflict harm on anyone. Family constellations address ancestral pain and its influence on our life today from as far back as five generations. Deceased family members' resentment and pain can be carried by someone today.

Testimony of Pat: The removal of her parent's demon.

I was introduced to Angel through my friend who knew of his extraordinary talents at working with the Light to make substantial life changes. My family has experienced years of family trauma where darkness had come over me and my children. For a period of three years, it felt as if there was no joy or lightness around our family. In that time, my youngest child had been diagnosed with PTSD related to an early childhood experience. His behavior and actions were impacting my other children and really affecting all the relationships in the family. We had tried therapy, medication, and so much for my son but nothing was working.

I went to Angel thinking the healing was for my son, but as he started working with the Light and healing him, he encountered that there were specific demons and dark forces around me trying to cause me and my family harm. He asked if I knew anyone who might be trying to hurt me? Immediately I did think of someone and produced a photo, he confirmed that it was exactly the person he saw in his vision. The healing shifted to be a healing to protect me, and from that protection protect my family.

We worked with the Light, and he showed me how to create a protection layer. After that session I felt a real shift. I invited each one of my family members to have their own healing with Angel, and one by one he worked with each of my children and also my husband. He was able to work with young children, teenagers, and adults. He has a way of being approachable to all ages. In his time with each of them, they expressed they felt connected with and understood. He gave each the Gift of how to work with the Light. Since the healings, a lot has changed in our family.

We are moving forward and onwards. The energy of each one of us has been profoundly changed. I am deeply grateful to Angel and to my friend for making the introduction and giving me the courage to seek him out.

Evil and Hate

I have told Erica that all of us are inherently Divine and born in love, so she asked me how people transform into evil beings. The answer came to me from the Gift as this scene: There was evil, and there was God both present. Every now and then, evil would snatch a soul and say, "This is mine." Like a predator, it made a random selection.

It would be challenging for someone to see their own possession, and they wouldn't have any tools to see or remove the possession. Most people don't know they're possessed. We have free will, but I think someone can be slowly trapped into possession. It escalates and affects them gradually. Some people find it amusing and enjoy being evil. I advise, of course, that everyone use the practice of protecting themselves with Divine Light through their Being of Light.

What about hatred? Hate is a tool for destruction. Erica asked me to ask the Gift about hatred and surprisingly one of the monsters communicated to me that hate is a tool to destroy things. It's a sentiment, but not an entity. Note, too, that rage isn't the same as hate. To really feel hatred, you must focus on it and work at it. Rage is not the same hate – it is a human emotion.

Erica also asked me to question the Gift about how we can remove hate. Children should be taught from an early age to connect to their Beings of Light and to act with love and compassion toward others. They need to be made aware that there's so much more in the universe than the material things they see around them. Our souls are just witnessing the hate. There is no judgment about it since they are simply witnessing human behavior. You think there is purpose in the current amount of hatred because you think that society will come back to being healthier. If there is no coming back, there is deterioration. Human beings can progress and move toward love and the Light…or humankind can choose to go toward the darkness since we have free will.

Erica wants to know what would then happen to the world. The answer I am given is that it re-starts, or it self-destructs. Maybe it will rise like a phoenix and restart, or it is the end. It will be what it will be. I do not understand why people can get so upset about things, or who said what, because it does not really have any bearing on the big picture. Societies focus has gotten minuscule, and the plot is lost for many. In the battle of good and evil (which is being fought right in front of us on the human plane), evil is winning by attacking the human beings that God has created, by using the energy of hate. Hate is coming from bad sources: evil. Evil sees a society that it can successfully spiritually attack. It is the same thing as a possession.

People get into so much darkness that they cannot see anything else, and they are blinded. Completely blinded.

Erica asks me how humans can transform from a Divine infant into an evil being. People are so angry right now and there is so much hate. Erica feels that she could easily name ten people personally that have a tremendous amount of hate in them, which they did not have five years ago. Anger and hate. She asks what the best way is to remove that hate? If the hate is purely an aggression from one being to another, that is one thing.

That is an issue for a psychiatrist. If the hate comes from a possession due to a bad energy, it will require some type of exorcism to remove it. The being could be trapped by this monster or whatever you want to call it. Therefore, it is out of the person's control, and they cannot control their own actions. These are two separate manifestations of hate. I wonder what percentage of the people with hate are possessed. It seems like there is more hate and it is escalating. What is the solution to remove this hate? It cannot be that you visit each person to remove it as it would take too long. Let's assume that you are correct and there is a lot of anger and hate. The only way I know to change that is surrendering to God, opening your heart to love and not being selfish. Preaching 'love more than hate' is effective. If a person were possessed, then this would require an exorcism.

A lay person would have difficulty identifying a demon, and it would be challenging for someone to see their own possession. If you are innocently attacked or possessed, you are a victim. That will affect your personality, your moods, and your actions. People will see the change in you, to sadness or anger or other negative emotions. I advise that everyone use the practice of protecting themselves with Divine Light through their Being of Light.

You can have a possession of a giant monster, and you can have human free will. Like when they talk about the little person on your shoulder telling you what to do, good and evil. It is an old wives' tale. Who are you going to listen to? If that possession is giving you bad ideas to do terrible things, (stealing, hurting others) you have human will to combat those desires. Depending on how strong of a person you are, your depth of faith, and how strong that entity is, Erica wonders if you can choose not to pursue that urge? I think you can be slowly trapped into it. It is not a moment that you choose to be one or the other. It escalates and affects you and then you find that it is amusing, and you like to be evil. You are then accepting and are open to the negative direction.

If this happens to a child, it is a tragedy. If that kid were a different kid with a different personality, the possession could have a different outcome. A stronger soul would be harder to possess. For example, if that child had a strong religious background or somebody intervenes quickly. It can then be controlled. Children should be taught from a young age to connect to their Beings of Light, to act with love and compassion toward others and be reminded that there is so much more to life that the material things that they see around them.

Erica would like me to ask the Gift what the end goal is for human life? To live like heaven on Earth, dwell in the Light, and remove all darkness? Do I think this enters anyone's consciousness right now? My answer is that people should have more of a connection to their Spirit. I have seen a blossoming of healing arts and believe that many people in our society are searching for and opening themselves up to a less materialistic and more spiritually fulfilling life.

Erica knows this is a very good time in the world to share something like this. It is an opportune time. People who are seeking to understand will find our book and be helped and I agree, but the question is…who genuinely wants to see it? Who wants to talk about demons and spirits? There is so much more than what we see. If you cannot make people understand that there is more, then they will stay with the nothing. If you can show them that there is, in fact, much more…they will want to learn in order to elevate themselves spiritually. They could become seekers. I am sure there are millions of people that are seeking the Light throughout the world. The more you learn the more you grow. Learning about my Gift requires a big leap into the understanding of consciousness and existence.

I ask you not think about evil on an intellectual level. Why? Because you are inviting, but not really inviting, but you are creating a dialogue of sorts. You should not mess with these energies. I know that I am protected, if not I would not be here right now. You are the architect writer who wants to chisel this down to the last detail. You chip away to understand everything. Do not even ruminate on these dark topics even though you are protected. Let this all go. Sometimes we do not need every answer for every question.

The Problematic Human Ego

Have you ever seen fights between parents while they watch their children play soccer? Winning becomes the priority, and they lose the point of playing a game. Wanting to win and have your name on a trophy is the work of the ego, not the pure Light-filled soul. The ego is part of evil and has nothing to do with our soul.

The ego must be controlled and managed. As a healer, I must combat my ego all the time. When I say I'm giving or doing a healing, I try to make people understand that I, as a human being, am not performing the healing but merely the conduit for it.

Humans are corrupted by their own ego, which leaves no room for unconditional love or selfless action. Listen to any conversation, and you can easily parse out the little comments that come from the ego. Ego is a form of negative energy that's a fluid, amorphic entity in the air. It feeds on humans in small bites, and it's another tool that evil uses to corrupt humankind. It's judgment and selfishness. To know ourselves better, we must leave our ego aside because it can distort our true perceptions. We should admit the uncertainties within ourselves and the world without the ego present.

8 LIVING AND DYING

Many people today live with the intense fear of death and dying. If people have only identified themselves with this physical realm during their lives, they fear the unknown that awaits them. They also fear the possible punishment that's often referred to in religious writings for wrongdoings during their life. The Tibetan culture instructs their children about the concept of death when they're eight years old, which I think is a wise practice. I remember one time I was running out of a hotel in Mexico during a business trip and I was racing to the airport to fly home. I had nothing to read so I asked the doorman if there was a bookstore close by. I hastily entered the shop and grabbed a book quickly from the shelf, which was the well-known Tibetan Book of the Living and Dying. I devoured the book during the flight. I loved that book and still do today.

In some healings, I can see that the person is going to die soon. This information is usually given to me when the person is ill, but not always. When I see that someone is going to die, I understand I must work with their Light Being and connect with their soul. I don't always tell a person that they will die. I'm always guided to provide words that offer them peace in a way they can understand. I work with Spiritual Light to create harmony for them, helping them to release fears, anguish, and other spiritual obstacles that may affect a peaceful transition. The healing involves preparation on a spiritual level, which allows the person to die with acceptance. Often, after the fact, the family will tell me their loved one died in peace.

How do I know someone will die? There are many different cases. I don't see the actual date of death, but I see the specific outcome and usually have a strong feeling about approximately when it will happen. Sometimes, I see that someone in my daily life is going to die, but I don't interfere. I saw someone the other day and was shown that they aren't well. It's a message, an instinct, and I can tell from the color of their skin or a look in their eyes.

In some instances, the outcome of the person's life can be changed. If they address a physical sickness early enough, adding non-traditional healing work to allopathic treatment, they create possibility for a different result. When someone has an apparently life-threatening illness, healing must become their top priority. Of course, the final outcome is always in the hands of God. We can never know what worked to save someone, whether surgery, doctors, praying, healers, or self-healing work.

When a dear friend came for a healing, I saw that he was going to die before long. It was ironic because he was healthy, while his wife was the one who was gravely ill at the time. His wife died shortly after I saw him, and five years later, he died at age 60. I played golf with him quite often, keeping my knowledge about his death to myself. I understood that I wasn't to tell him, but it was difficult for me to know this about my close friend.

When I worked in hospice, the patients already knew, of course, that they would die soon. I could see them fading away and becoming weaker energetically, as well as physically. In this case, the soul knows the person will die soon, so it starts to gently elevate from the physical body and begin the detachment process. The soul doesn't completely leave, however, until the moment of death. Suicide is a human decision that ends a physical life, but it doesn't kill the soul, which leaves at the moment of death and ascends regardless of the manner of death. I see that God views suicide with compassion.

I have seen many souls lifting and separating from their human body at the time of death. During the last moments of a human life, I see the Light-filled soul start to gently ascend from the horizontal physical body and elevate while rising upward into Heaven. Some souls come back for another new life experience, and some do not.

On the morning of September 11, 2001, Cathy and I were supposed to drive from Long Island to Manhattan, but we didn't head west after we saw the terrorist attack events unfolding on the morning news. We remained in East Hampton and drove into New York City about one week later. There's an incline in the Long Island Expressway from which we could see the first dramatic vista and skyline of New York City without the World Trade Center towers. I could see souls floating in the air above, disoriented and confused, and I knew they were lost. It was a heartbreaking sight.

One of the things I've learned as a healer is that when people die of natural causes, the soul is fully prepared to transition. I've seen souls slowly lift from bodies with the Beings of Light there to gently guide them. When a sudden accident occurs, the body doesn't know it will die suddenly, so the soul is taken totally by surprise. The soul is connected to the physical body, and it doesn't know what will happen in future moments. So sudden death causes a time of confusion, but eventually, all souls transition.

Healings After a Loss

I worked with a man who was terminally ill with a massive, inoperable brain tumor. His wife and several of his friends brought him to see me. He died after a brief time, however, and a month later, his widow came to see me for a healing. I immediately saw her husband above her as a floating ball of Light. "Do you talk to him?" I asked.

"No, someone told me not to communicate with him. I have to let him go, or he won't make the transition," she said. "He's right beside you. He'll leave the earthly plane when he's ready and in his own time. Right now, he wants to talk to you," I told her. She could feel his presence.

Healing of the Grieving Mother

At another time while attending a luncheon, the woman seated next to me shared that her seven-year-old son had died unexpectedly six months before. "Your son is in a safe place. Come to see me if you'd like," I told her. A couple of days later, she arrived for a healing.

"My son died six months ago, and I don't suffer from his death," she told me. She felt guilty and like something was wrong with her. "Do you dream about him?" I asked her. "Yes, I did, but one day, the dreaming stopped." "When you last dreamed of him, God gave you a gift—a deep sense of peace.

God took your soul to witness the soul of your son." I then described to her the vision I had seen. I saw the scene of the coffin that held her son, and I saw her soul rising into the sky and reaching a place where her soul witnessed many comets like lights moving rapidly. Her soul gently lifted her ethereal hands as she saw and thanked the cosmos. God had allowed her to see and know the location and condition of the soul of her son. At that moment, she felt the joy and the knowing that everything was as it should be. It was a surreal cosmic scene that I had never experienced before or haven't experienced since.

Imagine the mother of a seven-year-old son who dies in a sudden accident finding complete peace just six months later. It was an incredibly profound experience and an extraordinary gift for the mother. For me, it was an honor to witness. The day after the healing, I called the mother to ask how she was feeling. "I didn't see what you saw, but through you and your reaction, I understood what you witnessed," she told me. She trusted the explanation I gave her and felt a knowingness that it was true. This relieved her of the guilt she had felt about feeling peace after her son's passing. What a beautiful way to view the passing of a loved one.

The Man who wanted to know when he would die.

Erica tells me that she mentioned our book to someone who is eighty-three years old, and his response was, "Oh good, I can get a healing and know when I will die! Then I can start to pack and label the boxes!" I could not understand his perspective, but that is where his current mindset is.

Well, he should start packing because it is going to happen. It is certain! As people get older, they start to question things. When some people reach a certain age, they realize they will not live twenty or thirty more years and the feel the need to get prepared. 'Prepared' means different things to different people.

9 LOVE AND PRAYER

When I ask the Gift to define love, the answer I receive is that pure love is 'when the person and their soul are fully open to unconditional love and Divinity. The entire human being unconditionally connects to the Divine, and there are no limitations, requests, or judgments.'

Love is pure and Divine, while hate must be created to exist. A human being must accept hate and actively work at the act of hating. It isn't a natural condition. We're born as pure beings, and pure Divinity is our natural state. A baby has unconditional openness to its mother, and the mother usually does as well to the baby. But the mother can learn what she has to do to take care of her baby, while the infant doesn't have to learn anything, as it has complete openness and a Divine connection to its mother.

The following is a conversation with Erica on the topic of love:

Erica: Does the amount of love change in the world? It seems like there is less love in the world right now.

Angel: Of course, and yes there is less love right now.

Erica: Is there a way to create more love?

Angel: Yes, I connected to the Gift and was shown a beautiful image of Jesus—the upper part of his body— with the message "Accept Jesus and Divinity." The image showed many material items on earth surrounding Jesus, but they were slowly disappearing. As people looked to Jesus, the material possessions moved farther and farther out of the scene. The answer was presented clearly to me: "Yes, we can create more love if people become more spiritual."

Erica: This is so fascinating because in our society right now, material things seem to be moving closer and closer to us.

Angel: Exactly. The scene that was presented to me was so beautiful and profound—a simple answer to a complex problem. It shows that true love and happiness won't come through the material. Profound love and joy will come to us through a deeper connection and total surrender to the Divine. The message I received was Jesus saying, "It's Me. It's Me." People must connect to the Divine through their own traditions and beliefs, however. For me, Jesus embodies God and connects me to the Divine.

Erica: So, when asked how to create more love in the world, Jesus said, "It's Me." Wow. This makes sense because Jesus is the human embodiment of God and the Divine connector.

Angel: Beautiful and profound, yet remarkably simple. He didn't say who He was. He just said, "It's me."

We sat in silence for a while feeling the grace of that profound moment.

How to Pray

Erica would like me to share 'how to pray' with you. Many people might describe prayer as getting on your knees and clasping your hands together to recite specific words. But I don't pray like that. The answer I receive from the Gift about prayer is that it's a connection or corridor to the Divine. When I pray, I close my eyes and connect through the center of my forehead. That area opens into vastness, and it's there that I connect with my Being of Light, Divine Beings, and God.

It's easier than you think. Sometimes, the most difficult part is to find a silent moment and quiet the mind. Once you achieve this, you can open the door that leads to the Divine with the key of your choice.

It may be a particular Divine Being or saint that resonates with you, or it may be something in nature that you see as Divine such as a beautiful sunset. Once the door is open, you're connected to Divinity.

Some people think that praying is done when you really need something or have a problem to solve. It's important to pray in those moments, but you must know how to connect deeply. There are a lot of techniques for meditation today, but meditation isn't necessarily Divine or prayerful. We must first ask how to get out of our own way. Low-level thoughts have to do with human material things, such as what we're going to buy when you go shopping. We can choose to focus on more spiritual thoughts like love.

Thoughts have levels of connection or openness to the spiritual plane. I like the word "openness" to describe this. At the end of the day, the more our thoughts revolve around the material world, the more we're influenced by the material world. If we elevate our thoughts to those that awaken feelings of profound joy and love, our heart opens, and we can connect to a higher level of consciousness.

Most people don't have the capacity to switch automatically from daily life to a meditative state without practice and transition time. Retreats are a wonderful way to learn to meditate and facilitate spiritual awareness. I'm talking about achieving a contemplative state of mind, which is a practice. Erica had a profound spiritual, meditative, and prayerful experience while at the ocean with her 13-year-old son. She thought about how beautiful it was to see him so happy, and she felt gratitude to be in the water with him. She was fully present and felt enormously blessed. She experienced a connection with the Divine that came through nature and the love for your son.

God is everywhere, and once we connect through higher level thought, we are with God. When Erica was at the ocean, she was connected to Creation, her heart was open, and she felt the grace that this connection brings. The more we practice, the easier it becomes. Erica could eventually look at the ocean and immediately feel that deeper connection with Creation. Looking at the ocean and frantically thinking, "I need my fishing rod" or "I'm going to use my boogie board" are surface-level thoughts.

It definitely helps to immerse ourselves in nature. We slow down and notice the grass, the flowers, the water, and the sky. We begin to notice how the flowers change and grow from day to day. When we do this, we slowly take ourselves higher and higher.

If we're in a factory or an office surrounded by people who are filled with hatred and negative energy, we must make a concerted, conscious effort to avoid being dragged down with them. In this situation, we have to work on our connection to God. We can say the Lord's Prayer ad infinitum, but if we don't focus on it or if we watch TV while we say it, the level of our thoughts won't be raised at all.

Because you're with God's Creation, nature is the perfect place to focus and clear your energy if you've been in a toxic environment. In nature, you are God's Creation existing within God's Creation. Sitting and observing nature helps to calm the mind, and you can feel supported by and connected to Divine magnificence.

Find a time when you won't be interrupted. Start with ten minutes of contemplating something that draws your attention. For example, observe a droplet of dew on a blade of grass or a bee taking pollen from a flower. Don't question it. If your mind wanders, gently bring it back to your focus, but don't put undue pressure on yourself. Simply focus, and you'll naturally settle into a more peaceful, grounded state. Gradually, you'll increase the amount of time you spend. Once you're able to sustain this contemplative state for a period of time, you'll find that the sense of calm will carry over into your busy daily routine.

The Use of Sound

Using sound or music can also help to calm your mind and facilitate a spiritual connection. I love listening to Devi Prayer, a hymn to the Divine Mother Akasha by Craig Pruess and Ananda Devi. My mind focuses on the gentle sounds, and I'm transported into a contemplative state.

Erica wonders about where sound comes from. I asked the Gift. The answer I receive is that there are ancient sounds that come from the universe and exist throughout all time and space. I have had a vision of sound coming from the stars. These sounds include gongs, bells, and whales singing. They are Divine sounds that were created for peace and contemplation. My friend, the late Dr. Mitch Gaynor, often used chanting and Tibetan bowls to help his patients heal. These ancient sounds quiet the mind and body. They regenerate our cells, as our cells feel and recognize their sound and vibration.

There are sounds created electronically in specific megahertz frequencies that attempt to imitate the natural ancient sounds. Some of the higher frequency Solfeggio sounds in 852Hz are remarkably similar to the natural sounds. Now think about the current music trends, the sounds, and the lyrics. Very troubling, don't you think? Many types of meditation use mantras, which can be words or phrases. Some have been used for thousands of years and are used for certain intentions. The focused repetition of the mantra is important to reduce the outside noise, quiet the mind, and assist your journey inward.

Visiting ancient religious sites can also be highly effective. There are many locations worldwide that hold tremendous Divine energy. If you try, you can find interesting sites to visit during your travels. Notice how you feel when you sit in these places and imagine historical scenes that unfolded there.

Alone Time

Of course, meditation requires that we spend time alone, so we must learn to be comfortable when by ourselves. It's very challenging for some people. Living alone and feeling alone are different, however. It's good to be able to be alone without feeling lonely. It's interesting to discover where your thoughts take you when you're alone. Can you be alone with your thoughts for a day with no interaction with others or technology? How long can you be alone? Becoming comfortable while alone under any circumstances is a greatly beneficial practice. Be alone in peace where your mind can float and become unaware of time. Humans by nature are social, of course, and we don't need to be alone all the time. But we must practice being alone with our thoughts for a couple of hours and see what happens. What issues come up? What happens when you try to control your thoughts?

Once you feel comfortable spending time alone, you can teach your children to be alone. Don't overschedule them. Let them have time to be by themselves and encourage time without artificial entertainment so that they can be with their thoughts and imagination.

I strongly recommend contemplative time spent alone, whether you call it prayer or meditation. Allow yourself to connect to the Divine in this way, and it will feel like prayer, whether you use words or not. It's a time to reconnect with your soul and who you truly are as a Divine being. The benefits of this simple practice are profound.

10 THE BLACK BALL OF FEARS AND OUR BOX OF BELIEFS

I spend a lot of time working with people who are consumed by their fears. Many people spend most of their day focusing on one fear or another that take turns occupying their mind and gravely impacting the quality of their life. Fears can be irrational, yet this doesn't mean they aren't real, as they affect millions of people.

Some of our fears come from incidents in our lives, while others develop without our understanding their origin. There's an elemental form of fear that comes to us when it sees an opening in our energy field. This type of fear doesn't start here and now with us. It exists and sees an opportunity for a human host.

Fears of abandonment, poverty, death, or failure can endlessly scroll through our mind, but if the phone rings, our fear thoughts can be interrupted. When we finish the phone call, the fear thoughts may come right back. Fears are immediately visible to me in a healing since I see them as actual entities. They're completely solid, black floating balls hovering above the person. They have an actual "essence" like the monsters I see, and I can't transform them or reduce their size. We can't change elemental fears into anything.

Most people have great difficulty individuating their own individual fears from one another, as they're all combined into their personal black ball that hovers above them on the spiritual plane. New fears can find a home within us and stay with us, combining with other fears that we've already attracted, which results in a growing black ball of fear.

Some fears are what I call "ancestral," while I refer to others as "common." Ancestral fears are ancient and have become enormous entities over many thousands of years. The elemental energy of fear transcends culture and our human concept of time. Four thousand years ago in Egypt, a new mother who didn't have enough food to feed her baby experienced the fear that her baby might starve. Today, anywhere in the world, a mother in a similar circumstance could experience that same fear. The ancestral fear of not being able to feed your baby will seek a frightened and fragile new mother and make that mother its host. Another ancestral fear is the soldier's fear of dying or being hurt in a war. You won't have that fear if you aren't involved in war where you're witnessing death and destruction. Fears can't come to someone who has never had that circumstance in this life or a past life. In a healing session, I do not go back in time to see where a fear has originated. There are healing modalities which focus on ancestral healing that go back in time. The only thing I can do as a healer is to help the person remove the fears and teach them how to keep the fears at bay.

Common fears are those that are within our control, such as the fear of flying or the fear of failing a class. Both have realistic solutions in this lifetime, and they'll leave when the person finds a practical way to solve the underlying issue.

I have developed a system to help people manage their fears. At the end of a healing, I explain to them that they have some fears that are negatively affecting their life. We then create a written list together, identifying each fear one by one. There's rarely just one. The lists usually contain at least four or five. Once we identify the fears together, we group them. If someone has a list of twenty, for example, we can reduce it to ten significant ones as we continue to analyze them. They are no longer part of one big ball of fears; they're separated into smaller issues.

If as an adult, you had to defend yourself against fifteen angry children attacking you with sticks, they would collectively beat you. If you had to fight them one by one, you would be able to take the sticks from them easily and prevail. The same is true with our fears. After we've compiled their list, I tell the person to bring a beautiful image into their mind. I want them to recall that image as soon as any one of their fears begin to take hold. By doing this exercise diligently, they can reduce the amount of time their mind focuses on fear. After a while, the fears stop coming.

I performed a healing for a woman who was so disturbed by her fears that she vomited on her way to the healing. She had a horrible childhood with a mother who wasn't present and a father who was a severe alcoholic. There was often no food in her home, so she always wanted to go on play dates to other children's houses, where she might get something to eat. I worked with her for six months. When we started with her fear list, she had twenty-seven. We analyzed each one, identified them, and put them into categories. This way, when a fear came to her, she knew exactly which one it was. She then replaced the fear thought with the beautiful image. In the beginning, it was hard for her to break the habit of allowing her fears to stay in her mind. But she worked diligently, and we spoke often to help her maintain her focus.

Then, a couple of months went by without a phone call from her. Suddenly, she called and said, "Angel, I'm so upset! My ex-husband had taken the children for the afternoon, and as I was working on the house, I spent 45 minutes with one fear in my mind before I realized it!" She was distressed that she'd allowed the fear to be in her mind for such a long time. It just goes to show how vigilant we need to be with our fears. The last time I saw her, however, she felt more in control and was incredibly pleased with her progress.

Our Box of Beliefs

Besides our list of fears, we each have what I call a "Box of Beliefs." In the beginning, when you're a baby, you don't have a box of beliefs. But slowly, as you develop, you add beliefs to your box, such as the existence of God, religion, spirituality, fears, and nature. Other people you interact with can influence your beliefs and affect what's added to your box or removed from it throughout your life. Your culture is responsible for many of the beliefs you carry, although you eventually create a belief system that's uniquely yours.

When I visited India, I was struck by the sense of peace that flowed through communities. We observed many families who didn't know where their next meal would come from, yet they were able to remain content. This shows us that their box of beliefs contained an acceptance and faith that situations were as they should be. The cultural belief in karma can center and balance a life filled with the difficulties of poverty. They can dwell in peace regardless of their karmic situation.

As a modern Western society, we tend to devote little time to reflecting on our beliefs, but we must examine them in order to see if they serve us or not. We need to ask ourselves questions like:

- What do I believe?
- What happens when we die?
- Are we alone in the universe?
- Does God exist?
- Do I believe in past lives?
- How do I feel about karma?
- Why do I do good things?
- What is a soul?
- Do I believe in reincarnation?
- Do I have a guardian angel or light being?
- Is there a heaven?

Unfortunately, all too often, it's only after a life-changing experience or a proximity to death that people contemplate these important questions. Yet, understanding our beliefs is essential to a spiritually peaceful life.

The creation of a person's box of beliefs starts at an early age. Your children will be in your home for only a fleeting period of time in their lives, but the seeds that are planted during that time are crucial. As a parent, we are the prime influence in the development of our children through the experiences and viewpoints that we share with them. Of course, technology, TV, music, and culture are also contributing to their box of beliefs, whether they're aware of it or not. We must understand that we're helping them create their own personal box of beliefs.

Cultures used to have a more cohesive box of beliefs that was shared within communities or tribes. Before electricity and technology invaded our consciousness, the yearning to understand the world around us was filled with storytelling and reading. Older family members shared stories with the younger generations about their life experiences, births, and deaths. Today, children have a vast amount of information to sift through with many more contributors to our box of beliefs than in ancient times when information was geographically limited. Also, survival depended on understanding and navigating the natural world. What we saw and felt in nature was a larger part of our existence.

When someone tells me they don't believe in God, for example, I ask them, "Do you believe that when you die, your body is just a piece of meat that's left to rot, and that's the end of your existence?" When it's put in that way, most people say "no" or "I don't know." I then start to lead the person in an exploration of their beliefs.

In my personal box of beliefs, I know that my soul will continue, and I know that what's left here on earth is my body, which is a shell made for temporary use so that my soul could have a human incarnation. Death is a huge component of our box of beliefs. COVID-19 brought the reality of death to many people who had never contemplated it. In our culture, people avoid thinking about it, as they fear the unknown. Having some beliefs about what the death process will bring alleviates those fears.

In the modern world, children are rarely exposed to the death of relatives. Old people die in nursing homes unaccompanied by their families, instead of at home. I have sat with many people as they were dying, and I've experienced the soul preparing to leave the body. I have observed the Light Beings arrive and the channel of Light that the soul ascends through. Those around a person who is dying peacefully can participate and feel the peace of the moment when the soul returns to the Divine. If we can get beyond our fears of the physical body's deterioration and follow the soul experience, it can be beautiful.

Frankly, if you don't have a personal understanding of death, you can't live a peaceful life. As people get to middle age, they've had a lot of life experience. If they haven't already, it's time to begin asking questions like "Who am I?" and "Why am I here in this life?" They can ask if there's something else after life. The more answers they get, the more questions will arise. Contemplating these ideas will allow them to slowly develop their beliefs.

With so much technology and information available at our fingertips, whether true or not, our world is increasingly complex. Our children need to be equipped with strong values and a spiritual belief system at an early age so that they can make choices without being influenced by social media and others who may not have their best interests in mind. Supervising our children in a conscious and deliberate way is exhausting but essential for their spiritual future, whether we believe in spirituality or not. We need to know what's in our children's box of beliefs, and the easiest place to start is to thoroughly understand what's in our own box of beliefs as a parent. Think about who and what are contributing to your children's Box of Beliefs.

11 HEALING OUR CHILDREN

When we're born, we're pure Light. Small children are completely open like empty containers. They're like sponges, absorbing even more than parents tend to realize. So, it's of utmost importance to consider what we expose children to. We must try to see the world through their eyes.

If you watch a child at two or three years old in a stroller, they'll notice everything around them from the streetlight to the homeless person, yet their parent may be talking on the phone. The parent will probably never discuss the child's observations with them, even though it would be beneficial to talk about it.

Parents also often dismiss it when a child talks about something they deem as impossible. For example, a child might wake up and tell his parents, "I saw Grandpa last night. He came to my room."

The parents may respond, "That isn't possible because Grandpa is in heaven." Instead, they could say, "Wow, tell me about it. What did you see?' The child may then elaborate and say something extraordinary like, "I was sleeping, and he came with a bright light. I could feel how much he loves me." That little parent-child interaction can affect the child's soul connection for life. The parent doesn't have to believe what the child saw, but it's better not to impose their own beliefs on the child or suppress the child's experience. The child may be able to connect to the afterlife, but if we tell them it isn't possible, we close them off on a deeper level.

Some kids are purely and naturally connected to nature, while others need more encouragement to appreciate it. As adults, we must nurture the connection with nature and encourage our children's connection with Creation. I suggest that parents spend time with their children exploring the plants, insects, mud, rain, snow, sky, seashells, and other aspects of nature. Allow them to have the sensory experience of playing with mud, feeling the smoothness of the scales of a fish, or the tickle of an ant on their hand. This should be an integral part of their development, as it connects them to the greater Divine network. We have a responsibility to facilitate a Divine connection for our offspring, which can result in a shared joy and sense of peace and wonder.

We can teach our children about nature, and they will learn to love it and make it their own. It may be easier to go to Disney World than to explore the mountains, but we can also fill the day with activities in nature.

It's helpful to limit the use of technology. It can be a wonderful thing, but it tends to pull us into an artificial world and away from the real world. If we want our children to develop a connection with the natural world and the Divine, we must teach them to use technology wisely. It's shocking how many children spend all day on their computers for their schoolwork and then play games and interact artificially with others. Parents should find activities for their children that don't involve electronics. These may include painting, collage, beading, clay work, games, or outdoor activities such as bird watching, exploring, playing games, and playing sports. Encouraging creative thought is key to one's inner development.

Children and Material Things

There are physical items that we need to live comfortably, but most of the material things we focus on aren't necessities. It's important to teach our children to limit their material desires and learn the difference between a need and a want. Of course, we can enjoy a new sports car, and our children can enjoy toys. But the novelty and happiness from these items is usually short-lived, leaving us wanting the next thing . . . and the next thing. As parents, we must learn to find fulfillment and profound joy beyond the accumulation of things. This prevents us from becoming dependent on the material.

Parents can teach their children by encouraging them to donate and participate in charities as a family so that everyone experiences the joy of giving. It's helpful, if possible, to travel to areas less fortunate than our own, where children can see how other cultures live. This will teach them to feel compassion for all people.

Teach your children that, 'We don't buy things just to buy things.' While in India, I saw a group of women making bricks in the scorching sun. They were content and at peace. I think it has to do with simplicity. They were living with fewer temptations, and their existence wasn't so desire-driven as it usually is in the West.

Encourage Family Dinners

Many people today have lost the consistent family mealtime, and if they do sit together, the TV and phones are still present. Creating a consistent dinner time without technology of any sort is important for the family unit. This time creates a space to strengthen communication and step out of our fast-paced life. I have found with my own family that mealtimes have often led to our most profound conversations, and as a parent, it's during those times that I delve deeper into what's going on in my children's lives.

Unfortunately, many schools have sports practices that encroach on reasonable dinner times. If parents are working full-time, it can be challenging to find time for a regular meal together. Racing through meals is unhealthy in every way. We become mindless scavengers. The inconsistent timing of meals also creates a dysfunctional relationship with food. We need to eat with gratitude and in a state of mindfulness whenever possible.

I also recommend going for a short walk after dinner. It reconnects us with nature and fresh air before we retire for the evening. Whatever you do, if you're a parent, find ways to nurture your children's spiritual development. It's vital for their overall health, well-being, and the journey of their soul.

12 ADVENTURES IN INDIA

In 2001, my friend Dr. Mitchell Gaynor, an oncologist at the Weill Cornell Medical Center, who has since passed away, asked if I would attend a meeting with a well-known Healer from Honduras named Juan Almendares and serve as translator for them.

At the meeting, Mitch spoke in terrible Spanish, asking Juan if he spoke English. "Yes, I'm a doctor," Juan said, "and I graduated from the University of Pennsylvania!" We laughed and realized that my presence there was unnecessary, but since I was so interested in what they were going to discuss, I stayed. Juan was a licensed, educated doctor who had become a healer in a poverty-stricken, remote area of Honduras because the local community couldn't afford to pay for formal medicines or treatments. He treated patients using all sorts of modalities.

Mitch explained his reasons for arranging the meeting and described a scene from his own childhood when he experienced the opening of his third eye at age three. He was able to see a tumor in his mother's physical body when he was just four, so his journey into medicine, healing, and oncology started then. Mitch used the modality of sound healing in addition to conventional medicine and Spiritual Healing.

He expressed his desire to travel to India and meet Sri Sakthi Narayani (Amma), the well-known guru near Vellore in southern India. Although Amma is male, he's referred to as "she," as he is the embodiment of the Mother Goddess Narayani.

Amma was in her twenties at this time but had already become known for her miracles, and people had started to visit her to receive blessings. Mitch showed us a picture of Amma and asked us both if we wanted to join him on his trip to India. I didn't hesitate. I had no idea why that first image of Amma attracted me, but the attraction was significant. I knew intuitively that I must go to India.

Sri Sakthi Narayani Amma was born on the third of January in 1976 with marks on her forehead and arms that signifiy, in the Hindu culture, that she was blessed. From a young age, she had a profound interest in spiritual life and performed many puja ceremonies. Puja is a Sanskrit word that refers to religious rituals and adoration of idols in Hinduism. These ceremonies are done in many locations with profound respect. Offerings are made of flowers, fruits, ghee, and herbs, and there's often loud music, chanting, and singing. The puja ceremony can be a surprising mix of chaotic, loud music, whilst a peaceful, meditative ritual performance.

When Amma was just 16 years old, she materialized a golden statue of the Goddess Narayani that is considered the energy of our universe. This Goddess can assist us in strengthening our connection to the Divine. "Materializing" is the act of producing an object that wasn't there before or transforming something into something else. Sacred "cum-cum" powder from the curcumin flower is often used. This phenomenon is rare, but in the last few years, I have seen Amma materialize numerous items.

Amma is considered an "avatar" in India. In Hinduism, it's believed that Divinity can appear in human form, and an avatar is a highly spiritual being that often has special powers. The avatar descends on earth at times of great unrest to bring peace and harmony while alleviating suffering and guiding humans.

I mentioned my upcoming India trip to Ron Young, who was a close friend of Mitch's. The first thing Ron said was, "Don't let yourself be impressed by the phenomenon. Be sure to find what's behind the physical phenomenon." At the time, I wasn't sure what he meant, and I had no idea what he was referring to.

Mitch and I planned our trip for May of 2001. Neither of us

had ever been to India, and Mitch was bringing along his son, Eric.

The following is a diary of sorts of my experiences on three occasions in India.

At one in the morning, after seventeen arduous hours of travel, we arrived in the city of Chennai. I was immediately affected by the crowds of people in the airport in the middle of the night. The men wore pants and white shirts, while the women wore brightly colored saris. The air was saturated by intense heat, and there was a distinct and intense smell of spices, animals, and humans.

A compact car was waiting to take us to Amma's ashram near Vellore. It was a chaotic three-hour drive with cars and motorbikes whizzing by. I understood why I had heard that car mirrors get chopped off by oncoming cars there! The barely two-lane road was incredibly narrow with people and animals wandering everywhere, and we often had to stop for cows on the road since they're sacred. When we arrived at the guesthouse, we were given new white cotton clothes to wear during our stay.

Early on, we were gathered in a small room with about ten people. It must have been hotter than 100 degrees. I was standing by the door to get some air when an Asian woman gracefully walked in and quietly sat down between an older Indian man and where I stood. In the palm of her hand, she held a beautiful red, fully open hibiscus flower. The old man slowly extended his right hand toward her with a slight nod of his head, and without hesitation, the woman placed the flower in his hand. He started a movement with the fingers of his left hand over the flower as if manipulating it.

In a couple of seconds, I saw the flower shrivel up and slowly transform into a golden ring with a large red stone. The old man gave the ring to the woman, and she bowed her head in thanks. No words were exchanged, and I was the only one in the room who witnessed it. I was astounded, as I observed my first materialization. I later learned that the old man had been repeating a mantra for forty years asking God to send Narayani Amma to earth. We were all in that little room with a dirt floor, waiting to see the then 25-year-old Amma.

Ten minutes later after the old man had transformed the flower into the ring, Amma passed through the room. We didn't speak, but we saw each other and connected. As she passed by me, I perceived a beautiful soul through my Gift.

The pujas are quite lengthy and happen throughout the day in the ashram every day of the year. They are an integral part of Amma's daily existence. In between the pujas, Amma visits with people privately or in small groups. There are various large open-air temples throughout the ashram with the largest, most significant one dedicated to the Goddess Narayani.

The first puja I attended was to wash the idol that Amma had materialized of the Goddess Narayani. Amma was sitting on a small wooden platform looking toward an altar adorned with colorful flowers everywhere, and roughly 100 people observed the ceremony while sitting or standing. People sang loudly and played instruments, while Amma slowly and methodically washed the statue. She moved with such harmony, grace, and peace, while taking the time to perform the important ritual. She had several jars filled with honey, milk, and other colored liquids that she poured over the idol. Then, she rinsed it with the water that she kept in a coconut shell, and the colors ran together and dripped down around the statue. She offered flowers to Narayani, lovingly placing them on the statue.

These actions were repeated several times for a few hours. At the end, she dressed Narayani and adorned her with flowers and jewels. This was the first time I attended a puja, and I hadn't slept much in two days. So, I was a bit impatient and still in my rushed Western mindset, "OK, wash it. Come on. Let's get out of here." I thought it was a monotonous process and wondered what we were doing there.

Later, before the communal breakfast, we followed Amma to the "Puja of the Fire." I enjoyed this puja more than the first one, as I was beginning to soften to the rhythm of India. The Narayani statue was always present at the pujas and stayed with Amma as she moved around the ashram. There was a neat pile of sticks that were all cut perfectly. Amma silently placed the sticks dipped in ghee (clarified butter) in an arrangement, prayed, and thoughtfully ignited a small ritual fire. She also tossed flowers gently into the fire as an offering.

I observed that her actions were done in a prayerful meditative state, and she almost appeared to be moving in slow motion. Holding a fan, Amma directed the white smoke to Narayani. There was blaring, wild music playing at most pujas, however, that didn't seem to blend with the serenity of the ceremonies.

On our first evening, we attended the auspicious "Puja of the Full Moon." We were invited to walk through the town in the front of the procession with about 100 other people. The whole community participates in this ceremony and brings offerings. I still didn't have the appropriate sandals, so I walked barefoot on the blistering pathways. The air was filled with an oppressive, sweltering heat, and my feet were in agony.

Everyone gathered in front of a large stage outdoors that contained an enormous cement fire pit. People dressed in festive attire lined up for blocks with their offerings. They passed these up to the stage where Amma tossed the bountiful baskets of food and bouquets of flowers into the fire. There was white smoke everywhere, but it didn't burn my eyes.

My senses were overwhelmed by the loud music, the heat, and the mixture of odors of food and fresh flowers burning. I felt strange observing this as a Catholic, and it was challenging for me to open myself to such unfamiliar religious practices. Although I couldn't comprehend the burning of so much abundance and sustenance in such an impoverished place, I patiently observed the scene. I came to understand that the actions, movements, and gestures were the ritual, unlike in my tradition where so much is about spoken prayers. Sometimes, after a puja, Amma used a microphone and spoke to the people gathered. Later, Amma told me not to worry if I didn't understand the significance of the pujas. "You will understand it all in time," she said. "The fire is food for the angels, and I talk to them during the ceremonies. And the blessed water you are given during the pujas is pure energy absorbed by the water." Amma communicated with Creation during the pujas, and we simply don't have the capacity to understand.

The second day, I had my first private audience with Amma.

Wearing an orange cloth wrapped around her waist and over one shoulder, Amma walked toward the stable where the sacred cow Andrani was housed. A pujati, one of Amma's helpers, approached me and said "Santa Maria," gesturing for me to follow him into the stable, where Amma was sitting in a wicker chair. I sat on the ground at Amma's feet. I wondered if I was being called "Santa Maria" by mistake since my last name is Santamarina.

Amma immediately wanted to know my impressions of India. The first thing I said was, "Very hot." She then asked why I was there. "I came to see you to receive your blessing."

"You have already been blessed. Your trip to India started a long time ago, and this is the precise moment for you to be here." Amma was referring to my soul's personal journey. She then spoke about the purpose of my life and my journey toward illumination, explaining the ascension and growth of a soul when it decides to help and serve in love. She shared insights on the higher purpose of a human lifetime.

"The essential objective is to realize the purpose of your life and be able to accomplish it. Many can't, many don't want to, and others want to but can't. The one who wants it and achieves it is blessed."

Amma then talked to me about greed and possessions, sharing a story of a greedy poet who had authored a poem for the king. The king wanted to compensate the poet with a small ring. The poet rejected the ring and asked for more land. The king said he would give the poet all the territory that he could walk from 6:00 at night to 6:00 in the morning. At 5:55 a.m. the next morning, he had covered a vast 15 kilometers. The poet knew if he ran even faster, he would get 16 kilometers. When he saw the marker for the 16 kilometers, he made a misstep, broke his hip, and died. The angels came to retrieve the poet, and they put him in an old cart with other people who had died. The man was upset and told the angels that he didn't want to die and be put in that cart. He argued and explained that he was materially wealthy because he had just won an enormous quantity of land. Someone then asked him for a coin, and he realized that he didn't have one. He then knew that there was no difference between him and the other people in the cart and that he was just another body. When you give to others, you feel happiness and joy. The happiness that you obtain is by the giving of happiness to others, and that is how the heart fills with joy, which results in one moving toward illumination and the absence of sin.

Amma's words are always with me. More than an hour later, which passed by quickly, she asked Mitch to join us in the stable. She talked to both of us about the differences between people who don't have any karma and those who do. Amma explained karma in this way: "The actions of a past life can impact the future incarnations of that soul. It is a cosmic law of cause and effect, where we all have the freedom to choose between good or bad, and inevitably, we have to assume the consequences for our actions."

Amma knows who has an abundance of positive karma and will continue to produce it. She redistributes this karma to the pujatis, who don't generate their own karma, as they live in service to Amma and the ashram. She can balance the karma on their behalf. Amma said that once her mission in this lifetime is finished, she will go. She said that God, the creator of the universe, couldn't manifest himself as such on earth because his Light would be too strong for humans to observe. That's why God finds human forms like Amma, who is the essence of nature, to manifest on earth. "Amma is nature. In Hinduism, nature is Divine, and Divine is nature."

Amma also said that any religion is inherently good because it's centered on understanding and communicating with God. At this time, I didn't feel attracted to the Hindu religious tradition, but I was receptive to Amma's profound teachings, and enjoyed her overall goodness, smile, and serene presence. During that first meeting, I asked Amma to help my daughter Sofie, who has difficulties with equilibrium and walking as a young child with cerebral palsy. Amma put a photograph of my family over her heart and said, "Amma take care."

The evening after my first meeting with Amma, I wrote in my journal: "It's impossible to describe that conversation. I was impressed by the utter transcendence of her words. Everything that I had read, developed, and learned about my Gift was a preparation so that I could understand this specific message at this exact moment." During the night, I would wake up suddenly and start writing again as I recalled other teachings that Amma had given me. For example, I was thinking about the process of illumination. She had said that the journey of the soul begins with the soul being born from Divinity. The eventual goal of the soul journey is the total return to the ultimate source or pure Divinity. The proximity of the soul to Divinity is a process. "When we are free of greed and full of joy and love, there is no sin," she said so eloquently.

The following day, I retreated to my bedroom to rest, but Mitch told me Amma wanted to see me. I started to think about whether Amma would ask me for a donation and how much was fair to give. When we got to Amma, the pujatis allowed us to go into a room in her private apartment where she receives people. I didn't know if she knew about my Spiritual Healing work, but Amma said, "You are blessed to serve." She opened a jar of cum-cum and put some on the floor. Very carefully, she moved her hand in the air and looked at it intently. At that moment and to my shock, a small golden statue about three centimeters tall was created from the cum-cum. Amma handed the statue to me and said, "This is Lakshmi. Lakshmi is the Goddess that symbolizes spiritual and material richness. I will give you a mantra to take care of the statue." She suggested I place my Lakshmi on a little silver plate and make an offering of some grains of rice on the plate.

The concept of materializing is complicated for Westerners to comprehend. However, this phenomenon utilized frequently by avatars isn't unlike the use of a calling card by ordinary people. We exchange calling cards to establish a baseline for conversing and doing business. When someone performs a miracle of materialization in front of you, the bar for the conversation is set extremely high. This person can create something out of nothing or out of a bit of spice powder. It's challenging to understand this seemingly foreign reality. At the end of our trip, we witnessed Amma materialize a beautiful strand of pearls, and she asked us to give it to a mutual friend in New York.

Amma talked to us about the road to service. Looking at me many times, she said that she chooses who comes to her so that afterwards, they will spread the message and do as much good as they can. She said I'd be guided by her and would receive the strength to find the road to follow. I felt blessed and honored that Amma would refer to me in that way. I saw it as an infinite privilege that she would intentionally guide me so that I could use my Gift as it was Divinely intended. She advised me, "You don't need to read any more books because your teachings are already done." It was helpful advice since I used to read constantly about spirituality and had a whole library at home.

That night, we followed Amma onto a rooftop where the air was much cooler. I gazed up at the enormous moon and sensed a powerful energy. It made me feel as if I were floating rather than walking on that rooftop. I was in total ecstasy in the presence of this great master. I whispered to Mitch, "What is the name of the little statue Amma gave me?" Amma was way across the rooftop at that point but answered in a loud voice, "Lakshmi."

The experience with Amma was so intense that it was impossible to sleep or even write in my journal that evening. I was emotionally overwhelmed. After all, I was a trader from Wall Street who had just discovered a year and a half prior that I'd been given a Holy Gift. The next morning, we went to a charity ceremony in the large temple where Amma was going to give bicycles and tricycles to disabled men and sewing machines to women for them to support their families. A man who had no legs had journeyed 20 kilometers on a bus to get a special tricycle that he could pedal with his hands. The government required that people put their name on a list beforehand, but this man hadn't done so. He was terribly upset since he didn't understand why he wasn't going to receive his tricycle. I felt so much sorrow for the man, but I knew intuitively that he would receive one somehow. I tried to reason with him and even gave him ten dollars. But lo and behold, at the end of the ceremony, there was one tricycle left because the man who applied for it was too overweight to use it. So, they gave it to my new friend. I'll never forget the look of genuine happiness on his face.

Amma invited us to accompany her to the food hall where community people in need were offered meals. We entered a huge warehouse where about 500 people sat in long lines on the dirt floor. The food was placed on a banana leaf in front of each person. Even though many of these people didn't know how or when they'd have their next meal, no one hoarded food or asked for more. The atmosphere remained peaceful.

We had lunch that day with Amma away from the ashram in the countryside surrounded by palm trees and her animals. Later, we walked to an irrigation well to pour water on our faces to cool off. There were many children around who surrounded Amma. The scene felt like one in the Bible from 2,000 years ago as Jesus and his Apostles had a meal with children in nature. Everything was perfect and peaceful—the children, the well, the pond, and the trees.

At one point, Amma held a small rabbit, which she gave to a little boy to hold. "If you hold the rabbit, it will strengthen your arms," she said to the boy. I surmised that the boy had trouble with his arms, and this was done as a form of healing. The next morning, I walked to a temple in another area with one of the other Western visitors. We passed by two women bent over in a pool of mud, making bricks. One of them looked at me and smiled. I realized that even in material poverty, we can find peace, joy, and a loving heart. "How different our worlds are," I thought.

During another meeting with Amma, I asked for her guidance to be able to help others. "Divinity, the force that flows through me, will orient your steps," she said. She took a string and tied it around my wrist while praying with her hands around mine and her eyes closed. She blessed me and put cum-cum on my forehead. I felt overwhelmed by Amma's profound sacred love in that moment.

Before Mitch and I left the ashram, Amma wanted to see us to say goodbye. She asked when we would return. "I'll return soon with my family," I told her. The ashram wouldn't let us pay for our food or hotel, and Amma asked Ramu, her principal pujati, to accompany us to the airport. Ramu laughed because a few moments before, we had been told that a "chauffeur" would take us to the airport. So, we knew it was an honor for Amma to ask Ramu to personally escort us. For a week at the ashram, Mitch and I were in absolute heaven with Amma. We were able to spend time with her continuously, which was a rare privilege, as there were many people who wanted her attention and blessing. Only a small group could be with Amma at one time.

In today's world, Amma is so well known that I would never get the amount of "Amma-time" I received on my first trip. There were only about 20 foreigners there, and now, there are hundreds or even thousands since the ashram and Amma's following have both grown enormously. I perceived several people at the ashram wanting to sit with Amma for the benefit of their ego, and the environment can become competitive for "Amma time." Humans can be in a beautiful, spiritual environment, but their egos can ruin and detract from the experience.

At the airport, Mitch and I talked about the intensity of the experience, including how Amma had treated us. There was turbulence during the flight, so I repeated the mantra Amma had given me, "Om Namu Narayani," which means "I surrender to the Mother."

India opened my vision enormously, especially in terms of my understanding of other spiritual capacities. The ability to surrender changes the way you live. I saw women there making extraordinary mandalas on the ground out of flower petals and colored powders that they would sweep away with a broom in the evening. There was no attachment to anything. When I was able to look beyond the rituals of the Hindu religion versus my own, the message was one and the same—to love others and serve selflessly. I looked forward to introducing my family to Amma at some point in the future.

As I conversed with Amma in that first meeting I thought about my daughter Sofie's difficulties with equilibrium and walking as a young child with Cerebral Palsy, I asked Amma to help her. Amma put a photograph of my family over his heart and said to me, *'Amma take care.'* Amma then taught me that the human being is the only living being that has the capacity to 'decide.' For example, the elephant cannot take care of his offspring more than the elapsed time that nature has allocated for that species. He also said the world would be a much better place if man would consistently serve others, he said *'There are some people who have the desire to serve that do not have the richness of spirit, and there are others who have the richness of spirit but not the desire to serve. The very few that have the wisdom and desire to serve are blessed.'* Amma said that I possessed the wisdom, and that I should teach.

Again, that night I started writing in my journal with my mind spinning. I would wake up suddenly and start writing again as I recalled other teachings that Amma had given me. For example, I was thinking about the process of illumination. She had said that the journey of the soul begins with the soul being born from Divinity. The eventual goal of the soul journey is the total return to the ultimate source, pure Divinity. The proximity of the soul to Divinity is a process. Amma had also said eloquently, *'When we are free of greed and full of joy and love, there is no sin.'* I noted that Amma called me 'Santa Maria'. At first, I thought she had misunderstood my last name, Santamarina, then I thought that Amma had made some connection to my Catholic tradition where 'Maria' was the mother as was Amma. She changed my name because she is Maria also, and Maria is Amma, and Amma is nature. In essence, Amma wanted me to see him as Maria, which is confusing because she was calling me 'Maria', which was Amma's way of connecting to the portion of Divinity within me which is connected to Maria/Amma. We all have Divinity within us, and we can identify in diverse ways with a variety of aspects of Divinity. Amma was specifically and deliberately connecting to the part of my soul which was connected to Amma, by going through Maria, which was my reference point as a Catholic. I found these messages from Amma so profound and rooted in an inherent truth.

Mitch passed away in 2015. In the years following our trip, he became quite close to Amma and visited India many times. Amma even made a trip to New York City and stayed with Mitch and his family. I often think of Mitch and our beautiful journey together.

Amma in Canada

Several months after that first trip to India, Amma was to be in Calgary, Canada, so I was able to travel there with my family and introduce them to her. We arrived in the evening to the home of our host, where Amma was already performing a puja in the middle of a large living room. At the entrance to the house, there were many buckets filled with beautiful flowers.

As we walked in, my then 11-year-old daughter Sofie took a flower from one of the buckets and said, "When I meet Amma, I want her to hug me." We quietly explained to her that Amma wouldn't hug her and that if we were, in fact, able to meet with Amma, we would sit on the floor at a distance because no one is allowed to touch Amma.

Sofie is strong-willed, however, and remained steadfast. "This flower is for Amma, and I'm going to hug Amma." We sat through one hour that remained of the puja and had dinner with about 40 people. When it was almost time for bed, Sofie was still tightly holding her flower for Amma, when we heard someone calling out, "Santa Maria! Santa Maria!" I gathered my family, and we followed the man into Amma's room. After greeting me briefly, Amma looked at the flower in Sofie's hand and asked, "Is that for me?" Sofie nodded, and Amma opened her arms, gesturing for Sofie to come all the way forward and sit on her lap. "Is this what you wanted?" Amma asked.

Amma then asked Cathy, "Why are you here?" "I'm here because I want to know God," Cathy answered. Without hesitation, Amma took a bit of cum-cum from a small bowl and asked Cathy to extend her right hand. She put her hand over Cathy's and made a sprinkling motion with her fingers for a few seconds, but no cum-cum fell onto Cathy's palm. Instead, Amma gently placed a small golden statue in my wife's hand and said, "You do not have to look any further."

It snowed all night long, and the following morning, Amma was outside praying and walking barefoot in the snow, wearing only the cotton cloth around her body like in India.

Second Trip to India

When we asked Sofie what she wanted to do for her twelfth birthday, she said, "I want to visit Amma's orphanage in India." So later that year, we ventured to India as a family along with our son Nick, who was ten. Although we had no idea if Amma had an orphanage, we gathered many gifts for the children at Sofie's insistence. She told Cathy that we should buy 100 of each item.

We were with Amma on the day of Sofie's birthday, and she asked Sofie what she wanted for her birthday. When she said she wanted to go to Amma's orphanage, Amma replied, "I do not have an orphanage, but you may go to the one that is nearby tomorrow. Amma will send ice cream for the children." We found out that there were exactly 100 children at the orphanage.

Our family visit to the ashram was a wonderful experience, and Sofie particularly established a special connection with Amma. I saw the two of them walking slowly in Amma's garden one morning, deep in conversation. One evening, someone asked Amma, "What do I have to do to be with God?" She said, "People have to think about God to be with God. Sofie is with God all the time."

Third Trip to India

In 2004, we returned to India to see Amma again and began our journey with a visit to Sathya Sai Baba, who was an internationally known Indian guru. At the age of 14, Baba announced that he was the reincarnation of Shirdi Sai Baba, and he was well-known for his materializations. Baba was much older and more well-known than Amma.

Our stay in Baba's ashram at Puttaparthi was difficult and particularly challenging with children. We had to wake up at 4:00 a.m. to get into lines where men and women were separated, and thousands of people pushed to get a glimpse of Baba. We were roughly shuffled into an enormous hall, and when Baba arrived, he traveled through the crowds in a golf cart, occasionally stopping to give out Vibhuti (ashes) or objects that he materialized from the palms of his hands. People took pilgrimages to Baba to be blessed, and on a festive day, there could be 600,000 people.

We didn't have a private meeting with Baba, but when we walked out of the gate to leave, I saw him from a distance. The vision of him somehow magnified for both me and my family, making it seem as though he was right in front of us. I think Baba saw us, too. We left Puttaparthi a few days early because it was so difficult, and our son Nick became ill. We were relieved to be back at Amma's ashram.

When we saw Amma and told her we had been to see Sai Baba, she said, "We are the same" because Amma and Baba are both connected to the Divine. In the puja the next morning, I was distracted by an agitated man sitting next to me, who spoke aggressively to his wife. Cathy later told me that the man had approached she and Sofie, saying he had something for them from Baba.

Later that evening, the man's wife approached us and asked us to come to their room. They introduced themselves as the Mandeer family, which is Baba's family, and they explained that Baba guided them. They didn't do anything without Baba's direction and guidance, so he sent them to Amma's ashram. "We have lingams that were materialized by Baba, and we'd like to share them with you," the woman said.

Sai Baba's personal explanation for the lingams is: "It is not possible for you to understand the Divine and gauge Its potentials or know the significance of It's manifestation. In order to bear witness to the fact that Divinity is amongst you, it becomes necessary for Me to express this attribute of Mine. Otherwise, the atmosphere of hatred, greed, envy, cruelty, violence, and irreverence will overwhelm the good, the humble, and the pious. The Lingam is a symbol of the Beginningless and Endless or the Infinite. Its shape is like a Nirakaar. 'Li' stands for Liyathe, meaning 'That in which all names and forms merge,' and 'Gam' stands for Gamayathe, meaning 'That towards which all forms proceed.' It is the fittest symbol of the Omnipotent, Omniscient, and Omnipresent Lord. Everything starts from it, and everything is subsumed in it."

We visited with the Mandeer family for hours, and as we were leaving, Mrs. Mandeer exclaimed, "One second, one second! A message from Baba!" Suddenly, a letter from Baba materialized right in front of us. Baba communicates with the family by manifesting handwritten letters in this way. The writing is always in green ink and on the diagonal.

Mrs. Mandeer went over to one of the lingams, picked up a folded white sheet of paper, and began to read out loud: "To the Mandeer Family. . ." We didn't understand everything she read, but at the end, she read: "Baba sent you to Vellore to meet Sofia and her family. Baba loves her." It was so powerful. We had never introduced Sofie by her given name, Sofia, yet Baba referred to her by name in his letter.

When we next visited with Amma, we excitedly shared our amazing interactions with the Mandeer family. "Because of your experience in Puttaparthi, Baba came to you here," Amma said. Even though we never actually met Baba, he sent this family 400 kilometers to meet us on his behalf. Even though I have been to India three times, I've never been to the Taj Mahal, Jaipur, or other areas where tourists go. People are so surprised when I tell them I stayed at an ashram. Many people go there but never truly experience the culture. I believe there's much to be learned from exploring the culture and complex traditions of the people in India.

We took photos of one of the fire pujas, and a few of the images had hundreds of orbs in the background. When we blew them up on the computer, they looked like mandalas with complex geometries filled with a myriad of colors. Years later, when I saw Amma in New York, I asked about the orbs in the photographs. She said that in those pujas, the offerings are for the angels. "Sometimes, they are so happy, they show themselves."

Reflections on India with Erica

Erica asks if Amma feels my presence right now, at this moment as we write? I tell her that I can feel her Divine presence with us right now as we talk. Right here in my heart. When there is a strong connection, Amma certainly feels it.

Erica wonders if I am able to connect to Amma when I want or need to. We are describing communication on another level or plane that we cannot perceive or comprehend. Right now, in this moment, I feel a deep peace, humble respect, and abundant love. I do connect to Amma often, but this moment is particularly intense because I am reading my experience to you out loud, I am intently focusing on Amma and my experience in order to convey it to you for the book. It is extremely powerful because I am going exactly where I want to go spiritually to explain what needs to be explained to you. To connect with Amma and feel this elevated level of intensity, I am now going to start rereading this journal because I realize it brings me right back to the transcendent moments in the presence of Amma.

Erica wonders what she will feel when she sits alone, focuses, and writes this session out. One's connection depends on how you read it, how much time you dedicate to it, and where you are in your current soul development. The message from Amma may not be meant for everyone at the precise moment that they read this chapter of our book. I think Amma communicates with different people in diverse ways. In the puja ceremonies, he demonstrates his innate Divine nature to the participants who are observing in a connected way. In my own case I was fortunate to have direct personal conversations with Amma, however I initially had a strong connection to Amma from seeing his photograph. People may connect to Amma just from reading about her.

Comment from Erica:

'As Angel walked out of my pebble garden where we sit together, he turned to me smiling and said, *'Amma is with you now. You can ask questions.'* I had no idea what he meant and did not feel any different, until I sat down to write a few hours later...I then began to feel love radiating outward from me with such power. I felt like I was surrounded by a bubble of emanating intense love that was the size of a Volkswagen Bug. All I could think, and feel was...Love, Love, Love, for absolutely everyone and everything.

13 FINAL THOUGHTS

I had wanted to write this book for a long time, and I'm grateful to Erica for offering to help me. My hope is that reading these pages has helped you better understand the complexity of our existence in the universe and that there exists a Divine force that influences our lives.

I feel that since I have been blessed with this Gift that gives me access to so much information about the spiritual world, it's my responsibility to share it with others. I feel an obligation of sorts. Erica requested that I ask the Gift to explain in simple terms the most important message to be conveyed to people at this time. The answer I received was this: "Light. The existence and power of Light. Spirituality and Light."

Spiritual Light can help us heal ourselves and others. It is Grace coming from the Divine for our benefit, and it fortifies our connection to the Divine. As humans, we have a desire that pushes us to continue searching for the mysteries of the infinite truth even though we often don't know what we're seeking. But the process of spiritual growth develops in a parallel field to our human lives. There are stages of spiritual development that aren't consistently timed or linear because of the interference of our daily lives, especially since most of us don't live in a cave in Tibet immersed in divine discipline.

Months might pass with no extraordinary spiritual experiences, and we may feel that we aren't growing at all during that time. But then, suddenly, a book or conversation can illuminate our thinking. Of course, what I've learned is that the essential part of life as a seeker of the truth is to remember that it's about the search, not the destiny. We never arrive at an end since absolute "truth" is infinite. Our true journey is about enrichment and growth, and our search is altogether personal and requires our deeply intimate dialogue with God. And the advent of our search can start at any age or stage of life. Once you open your heart with love and start looking for the truth, material things and your day-to-day busy life will lose its importance. You'll continue to live your life, but your connection to the Divine and the spiritual world will take over. Your life will take on new meaning. This reliance on the Divine as a source of guidance for your destiny is what will lead you to fulfillment. The ultimate goal is to totally surrender to the Divine.

Creation put you in this place and time for a purpose. Your destiny has led you to live in your current environment and not the cave in Tibet. Your challenge is to grow and expand within the parameters of the life you have now without wasting this precious incarnation.

You can incorporate these principles into your life and accept these truths that are beyond intellectual comprehension. You can begin to recognize and then utilize your own Gifts. Once you deeply understand that there's so much more, and you open that conceptual gate, you'll realize that the journey is what's important—not the destination. Become a seeker of the truth, and you will also see better with your eyes closed.

"I surrender to the Divine."

EPILOGUE: MEETING SEBASTIAN

By Erica Broberg Smith

As Angel and I neared the end of the book, I told him I was worried about creating a profound ending that would wrap up the message in a beautiful way. That evening, before I fell asleep, I prayed and asked Jesus how I could ever thank Angel for sharing his journey and Gift with me.

The writing of this book has changed me profoundly in so many ways and proven to me without a doubt that all the ideas I suspected about my existence, heaven, and the spiritual realms are true. In that quiet moment, I asked God to help me say thank you to Angel, as I couldn't think of a meaningful enough gift for him.

After I prayed, I couldn't sleep. My mind wandered and started to contemplate the connection between Ganesh and Jesus. Did they know each other? I sat up, opened my iPad, and searched the words "Ganesh and Jesus." The first item that came up was a website called "Choose Only Love." I glanced at the description and saw the mention of Buenos Aires, which caught my attention since Angel is from Buenos Aires.

I began to read about a man named Sebastian Blaksley, who has been receiving messages from the Divine realms of Angels since 2018. Suddenly, I was covered in goosebumps. I had stumbled upon some sort of connection. I texted the link to Angel to share my random discovery. Soon after, I fell asleep. The next morning, Angel called me in shock and shared with me what had transpired earlier that morning. When he saw Sebastian's photo on the website, he immediately felt a connection. He could tell that Sebastian was a good and honest person.

Sebastian had been in an auto accident in Argentina in 1973, which was when his communications with Jesus began. That was the same year as Angel's accident in Argentina. So, he sent a message through the website, requesting to speak with Sebastian. He asked if Sebastian's car accident was between the towns of Del Viso and Lujan, which was where Angel's accident had occurred. Five minutes later, a man named Miguel called Angel and confirmed that Sebastian's accident happened in that area. Both accidents involved a railroad track.

Sebastian called Angel shortly thereafter, and they figured out that their accidents happened in the same intersection of road and train track. Angel explained that when he and his father drove to their farm, they had damaged both tires from hitting a hole in the pavement alongside the train track in that spot. The nearly fatal accident happened on the return trip from their farm to Buenos Aires. Sebastian's accident occurred when his mother drove into a train. One brother tragically died in the accident, and Sebastian lay under the train for a long time. He received a message from God telling him not to move and that someone would come and get him.

Angel and Sebastian also discovered they had been taken to the same hospital. Both of them studied business administration at the same university in Buenos Aires, and they both went to the U.S. later to study and work. Their spiritual awakenings happened separately, but they both received a calling to serve God.

The connection with God had been there for both of them since the time of their accidents, but they didn't dedicate their lives to healing and sharing the message until they were both in their forties and had left their traditional business occupations. Angel asked Sebastian, "Why do you think this happened to us both and that we're talking to each other now?" Filled with emotion and love, he replied, "Angel, Lujan is a holy place!" There's a massive basilica in Lujan dedicated to The Virgin of Lujan, and there is a yearly pilgrimage to the basilica. They talked about the concept of surrendering to God and leaving their Gifts in the hands of God. Sebastian shared with Angel that he felt frustrated and pressured to "do more," and Angel shared with him that he struggled with the same feeling. Sebastian received a message from Jesus that explained there was nothing "to do." We just have "to be." Sebastian told Angel that the Virgin Mary didn't have to actively do anything. Why didn't she tell Joseph that she was expecting Jesus? If God wanted Joseph to know, He would have told Joseph. Mary was completely surrendered to God.

Angel often says to himself, "It's in the hands of God." Sebastian and Angel have already had many conversations, and they'll continue their Spiritual Healing journey together. It's a beautiful connection made in the realm of heaven—a gift for them both.

AFTERWORD

Historical Precedence for Charismatic Gifts
By Angel Santamarina

Shortly after I received my Gift, an Argentine priest named Father Manuel Prieto Garcia graciously met with me. He explained the Catholic Church's stance on charismatic gifts and shared his research with me. His thesis, Los Charismas en la Iglesia, encompasses more than 400 references for Holy Gifts. To understand my Gift from the point of view of the Catholic religion, I will summarize the writing of Padre Manual Prieto Garcia, as I understand it.

Many scholars of the Bible have specific ideas about Holy Gifts, and superb theologians analyze every written word. The Bible is the anchor for Christianity, and when we read phrases in the Gospels where Christ instructs the Disciples to go and rid people of leprosy and demons, it confirms that what I'm doing has already been done. It's nothing new.

In the Bible, Paul discussed Holy Gifts in the first letter to the church at Corinth, 1 Corinthians 12:1-11, and in 1 Corinthians 12-31. He mentions nine specific Gifts: apostles, prophets, masters, miracles, healings, assistance, government, tongues, and interpretations. Apostle Paul tries to express them in these defined categories, although they can be combined and overlapped. The charismatic Gifts are for all to share.

Throughout the centuries, many religious orders have analyzed and studied these Gifts or charismas. Pastoral theses have been written about one Gift or another. These charismas granted by Creation have been given to many laypeople around the world throughout history. They weren't reserved solely for priests or ministers. The Catholic

Church describes the Gifts that I believe I've been given as the Gift of knowledge and the Gift of healing.

Others may receive different Gifts of varying magnitude, but we must all surrender as channels for the process to occur. The Gift of knowledge is a supernatural revelation of circumstances of the past, present, or future that we can't know through human reasoning and comprehension. This Gift provides fragments of knowledge that give light to the eternal truth. The Holy Spirit decides the exact information that is needed for a person or their circumstance to help them grow. This transference of knowledge comes through me during a healing. I don't need to know any details about a person's life before I perform a healing since the information I receive is from a higher spiritual plane.

Father Garcia suggested that I explore the works of Father Emiliano Tardif (1928-1990), who was a prolific spiritual writer. His books are widely available in both English and Spanish. He explained that Jesus performed healings as a proclamation of the word of God. This is a way God proclaims victory over sin and the consequences of sin and sickness. Suffering, sickness, and death came into the world as a punishment for man's original sin. If a three-month-old child becomes gravely ill, he hasn't committed any sin. It's because he belongs to the human race and has inherited the consequences of original sin.

When Jesus healed others, it was a reminder to us that He has power over original sin. When Jesus resurrected someone, He was again showing power over original sin. The resurrection is a symbol of His great victory over original sin. It's important to explain to our families that there will be a final salvation and freedom from original sin for humanity. Our salvation is a core belief that gives meaning to our lives.

What is the point of original sin? The Gift says we failed God. It was a beautiful scene, and God was there. I was given an image of God with Adam and Eve and the tree. There was this impulse or sentiment of "We don't need God; we're going to eat this." It was a smug feeling of control. We have failed God as a race, and we're collectively paying the debt for that failure. I've been shown that humans are an experiment for just a limited time. We're just a small piece of God's vast work. Humanity will end eventually and be completed, but the universe and Divinity will continue on. Father Tardif commented: "Sometimes when I finish leading a mass, people will approach me to lay my hands on them and say, 'Father, please put your hands on me.' I feel like punching them because I just told them all to give God the time do his work. Spiritual Healing does not require a touch as it is not transmitted that way. Remember that when Jesus entered Jerusalem, he was riding on a donkey. If you touched the donkey, you would receive nothing. I am the donkey." The use of the Gifts requires total faith and surrender. The Gift of knowledge gives me no doubt in the information I share. I know the information is the irrefutable universal truth.

Father Tardif explained that receiving a charisma is proof that we by ourselves can't do the healing work. It's very humbling to know that I can't heal someone. I must accept my weakness and accept help. In accepting the charismas, you must "die on yourself" and leave the opinions of others behind. You can't proceed with the use of your Gift and believe what others say about you. You must surrender to your mission. Worrying about what others say or think puts out the fire of your spirit. You must decide that your reputation isn't important and know that the kingdom of God is above all.

There was a time when I was afraid to tell anyone about my Gift, but I'm no longer concerned with the opinions of others. I have my work to do, which is out of the reach of human reasoning.

APPENDIX A

<u>Questions for Discussion</u>

- What was your favorite part of the book and why?

- Are you afraid to die? If so, can you explain why? If you aren't, can you explain why?

- What do you believe is true about the relationship between Jesus and Ganesh?

- Where do you think the soul winds up eventually? Does it ever finish its journey?

- Have you ever met someone you think has a monster attached to them?

- Who do you think the Grey Beings are in Lucio's healing?

- Did your parents or grandparents speak to you about the spiritual world when you were a child? If so, what did they say?

- Do you pray?

- Have you ever felt a Divine presence?

ABOUT THE AUTHORS

Erica Broberg Smith

Erica Broberg Smith is a practicing residential architect the Village of East Hampton for twenty-five years. Her practice of designing houses for families has been a lifelong exploration of what it means to truly feel at 'home'.

She began professionally writing with a column called Foundations, in the East Hampton Star newspaper, in 2000. Foundations subjects ranged from construction techniques to architectural design and explored the humor that is often desperately needed when building a house.

Erica's spiritual journey began as a child, and she continues to explore the spiritual world today. Erica resides in beautiful East Hampton, New York, with her husband Scott, two children, three dogs and one cat.

Angel Santamarina

Angel grew up in Buenos Aires, Argentina. He came to New York in 1982 to work on Wall Street.

He later met his wife Cathy and had 2 children. In 1999 he had an experience that changed his life bringing to light insight that completely escape what people generally perceive. He later wrote a book Vivencias de un Sanador Espiritual." Experiences of a Spiritual Healer".

Angel has been helping people for over 20 years performing over 2000 healings.

RESOURCES OF INTEREST

Ron Young
www.healingwisdom.com

Hilda Charlton
https://www.hildacharlton.com

Daskalos, Stylianos Atteshhilis (1912-1995)
https://anthroposophy.eu/Daskalos
Kyriacos C. Markides: 'The Magus of Strovolos' (1985)
Daniel Joseph: 'Swimming with The Whale' (2012)

Barbara Brennan Institute
https://barbarabrennan.com

Dr. Bert Hellinger
https://www.hellingerdc.com

Yogmata, Keiko Aikawa
http://yogmata.com

Sri Shakti Narayani Amma
https://www.belovednarayani.org

Sri Sathya Sai Baba
https://www.sathyasai.org

Sebastian Blaksley Healer
https://www.chooseonlylove.org

Contact Information for the Authors

Angel Santamarina

Email: santamarinaangel@gmail.com

Website: www.angelsantamarina.com

Angel resides in East Hampton, New York, USA, and Uruguay

What's App: +1-631-353-8066

Erica Broberg Smith

Email: erica@ericabrobergarchitect.com

Website: www.ericabrobergarchitect.com

Erica resides in East Hampton, New York, USA

Instagram: @IseeBetter2022 and @EricaSmithArchitect

Made in the USA
Middletown, DE
26 March 2023